Bu No Michi
My Journey Through Okinawan Karate

Hanshi Robert Teller

Bu No Michi: My Journey Through Okinawan Karate
2018 Robert Teller
Pottstown, PA

Bu No Michi: My Journey Through Okinawan Karate
Copyright © 2018 Robert Teller
ISBN-10: 1722830832
ISBN-13: 978-1722830830

Cover design by Lloyd L. Corricelli
(www.authorlloyd.com)
Edited by Robert Sterling and Lloyd L. Corricelli
Proofread by Lloyd L. Corricelli and Robert Sterling

ALL RIGHTS RESERVED. This book may not be reproduced in whole, or in part, by any means, without the written consent of the publisher.

Any trademarks referred to within this publication are the property of their respective trademark holders. None of these trademark holders are affiliated with Robert Teller.

All photos are the property of Robert Teller and may not be reproduced without his written permission.

ACKNOWLEDGEMENTS

There are literally hundreds of people without whose help, advice, knowledge, and hard work I could not have produced this book. I don't have space to list everyone by name, so if you provided material assistance and you don't see your name listed here, please accept my heartfelt apologies and know that I have not forgotten you.

Thank you…

First and foremost, my beloved wife Kiyoko Miko Teller, and her very patient parents, Toyoko Chinen and Kotoku Chinen.

Then (in no particular order): Master Masanobu Kina's daughters Yoko Kina Yada and Emiko Kina; Dr. Warner's daughter and son, Irene Yomoe Cooper and Ion Masashi Warner; My sister-in-law and brother-in-law, Akemi and Ron Nix; Jim Logue; Cezar Borkowski; Steve Mullahy; Dave Bardi; Connie Colosimo; Pat McGale; John Anthony; Kathy NcCrea; Masako Scott; Tako Tursi; Lloyd Corricelli; and Robert Sterling

In a world full of "information," few remarkable individuals actually possess genuine experience based knowledge. Robert Teller Sensei is a remarkable martial artist with years of practice in Okinawa and teaching in the USA.

He is one of the very few 'foreigners' who actually witnessed the twilight of Karate's golden age.

Cezar Borkowski, Toronto, Canada.
Okinawa Karatedo Kyudan, Hanshi Ryukyu Kobudo Kyudan, Hanshi

Contents

MY INTRODUCTION TO THE MARTIAL ARTS - 3

HOHAN SOKEN AND FUSEI KISE - 19

SHUGORO NAKAZATO - 35

MY RETURN TO THE UNITED STATES - 48

BACK TO THE SOURCE - 58

THE PICTURE OF SHOSEI KINA - 98

MASANOBU KINA - 113

DR. GORDON WARNER - 128

SHIAN TOMA -132

TAIKA SEIYU OYATA - 140

THE WRAP UP - 152

Foreword

My name is Tetsuhiro Hokama, I'm seventy-three years old and I'm a Tenth Dan Hanshi in Okinawa Karate Gōjū-ryū. I have a PhD in Physical Education. I'm also the owner of a Gōjū-ryū Karate Dojo and an Okinawa Karate Museum.

On behalf of Sensei Robert Teller, I would like to introduce everyone to this fascinating book called *"BU NO MICHI."* Five years ago, I had the honor of meeting Sensei Teller through a unique individual named Sensei Taika Oyata Seiyu. From that moment we have shared our mutual interest in Okinawa Karate history.

In 1965, after graduating from high school, Sensei Teller joined the United States Air Force. While stationed on the island of Okinawa he became very interested in Okinawan martial arts. Sensei Teller wasted no time joining a local martial arts class and immediately loved it. Over the decades he was fortunate to have studied under many Okinawan masters including Nagamine Shoshin, Hohan Soken, Fusei Kise, Sugoro Nakazato, Katsuyoshi Kanei, Shinyu Isa, Seikichi Odo, Masanobu Kina, Shian Toma and Seiyu Oyata.

Sensei Teller's military service on Okinawa gave him the opportunity to interview and write about many Okinawan karate masters through a local magazine. His journey in Okinawa karate is unique. Sensei Teller may be from a foreign country but his Okinawa knowledge is amazing.

This book, "BU NO MICHI," gives you a rare opportunity to look into the world of Okinawan karate masters through his personal experience. This has become Sensei Teller's mission: to pass down the real history of Okinawa Martial Arts for everyone to enjoy.

It's with great pleasure I recommend "BU NO MICHI" to the world. I truly believe this book will go down being a great masterpiece of Okinawa Karate history.

1

MY INTRODUCTION TO THE MARTIAL ARTS

It was June of 1965, and I was excited – my cousin Frank was coming home from his tour in Japan. He had enlisted in the Navy a couple years prior, and I was really looking forward to seeing him. Frank was kind of a role model for me; he was three years my senior and I had always looked up to him. And since I had just enlisted in the Air Force, I wanted to talk to him about military life and get a sense of what I was getting into.

Frank told me a bit about the military, but he said the Navy and the Air Force were entirely different experiences, and I'd mostly have to wing it. It was a bad joke but I laughed anyway.

He did give me one thing to think about. While he was stationed in Japan, Frank had earned a black belt in aikido.

"In what?" I asked.

"Aikido. It's a Japanese martial art."

"Like fighting?" I asked. "How does it work?"

"I'll show you. Attack me."

"Attack you? What do you mean?"

Frank was beginning to lose patience. "Punch me. Grab me. Attack me."

I wasn't mad at him and I didn't want to hurt him, so I threw a half-hearted punch, which he slipped easily."

"Come on, little girl. Attack me. Like you mean it."

Okay, now I *was* getting a little angry. "Little girl?" I thought. "Okay, Frankie, dodge this." And I lunged at him, throwing my best left hook at his head. Next thing I knew I was looking up at him from the floor, and he was laughing at me.

"Come on, *Roberta*! Is that the best you got?"

"Okay, Frank, you got lucky." And in the same motion as getting up, I launched a real attack at him. I was pissed! I hit the floor a little harder that time; it knocked the wind out of me and I was struggling to take a breath.

"You okay?" he asked, as he bent to help me up. "Hell yeah," I said. "But you won't be!"

I was determined to wipe the smirk from his face. I swung at him with everything I had, and found him standing behind me with my arm wrenched uncomfortably toward my head. When he let me loose I attacked him again. I tried every type of attack I could think of, from every direction, as Frank turned every one aside with ease. After twenty minutes I was too tired to throw another punch. Frank had hardly broken a sweat.

"That," he said, "is aikido."

All I knew at that moment was that I wanted to learn it.

I was inducted into the Air Force just two months later, in August, 1965. My basic training and tech school were pretty uneventful, and in December I was assigned to Naha Air Force Base in Okinawa.

The author, Robert Teller reminiscing with cousin Frank Bunting.

"Wow!" I thought. "Okinawa's part of Japan! I can study aikido!" So I contacted Frank.

"Frank, I'm going to Japan. Well, Okinawa. Do you know anywhere near Naha I can study aikido?"

"You're kidding, right?" Frank replied.

"No, why should I be kidding?"

"Because Okinawa's the birthplace of karate. Forget aikido. You'll have opportunities to study with the most amazing martial artists in the world. Living legends."

I can never repay Frank the debt of gratitude I owe him. That day he helped put me on a path – a martial arts odyssey that set the course for the rest of my life.

MY JOURNEY BEGINS

I'll never forget flying into Kadena Air Base, and then riding the bus to what would be my new home, Naha Air Base. It was a Sunday morning, and as I looked out the bus window I felt like I was watching a movie. I saw an old man pulling a rickshaw full of vegetables, old women carrying baskets of produce on their heads. And I'll never forget the distinctive smell of the *ebinjo* ditches that lined the road, where people squatted to relieve themselves with no self-consciousness or embarrassment. It was an amazing new world to me – like a journey to Oz.

Binjo ditch to the left of the picture

When we arrived at Naha Air Base, we were informed that we'd be briefed and processed in on the following morning and cautioned not to leave the base. I tried to occupy myself around the barracks, but I've always been a restless sort, and by mid-afternoon I could no longer contain myself. I wanted to explore this new world, but I wanted company. So I told one of my fellow recruits that I couldn't wait till the next morning and had to go downtown and see Naha City today. We snuck out the back gate and hailed a cab. Only one problem: the taxi driver spoke no English and we spoke no Japanese.

I tried to tell the driver we wanted to go to the nearest karate school, but he didn't seem to understand. I kept repeating "k'roddy! K'roddy!" while making chopping motions with my hands. Finally, he figured it out.

"Ah," he said with a smile, "*Kara-te*," emphasizing the correct pronunciation.

"Yes. That's what I've been saying!"

"Dojo," he said.

I replied, "Yeah, whatever."

The driver took us to the middle of Naha city and dropped us off at a dojo. It was full of spectators. Apparently, every Sunday evening busloads of Japanese tourists came to watch the

First day at Naha Airbase in Okinawa.

karate demonstrations. How was I to know that the sensei was Master Shoshin Nagamine, one of the most respected karate masters in Okinawa, headmaster of Matsubayashi-ryū karate?

We sat with the tourists, and I saw real karate for the first time. I watched in amazement as students kicked a heavy wooden block, about eight inches square and ten feet long, with their bare feet, full force. The wood had a slash down the middle and made a loud "clacking" noise each time it was kicked. Then they broke boards – *piles* of boards – with a single punch or kick. And bricks. Finally, they performed kata with breathtaking power and speed. The precision of their movements blew me away! So it was that I decided, in one night, that this amazing art would always be a part of my life. After the demonstration, I sought out a student who spoke English and told him we'd definitely be back.

We caught a cab, got back to base without much trouble (it was much easier to communicate "Air Force Base" than "k'roddy"), and managed to sneak back in undetected.

When we got back to base I couldn't wait to tell everyone what we saw. I said I was going to enroll the next day and I was met by a lot of skepticism.

"We're the enemy! Do you really believe they're going to teach you their fighting secrets?" someone asked.

"We're not the enemy anymore," I responded. "The war's over. It's peacetime."

"It's been less than twenty years. Okinawans have a long memory. Your teacher was a grown man while the Americans were still "oppressors". They may take your money, but they won't teach you anything worthwhile. They hate *gaijins*!" (Gaijin is the Japanese term for a foreigner, especially an American. It is not particularly complimentary.)

But I decided I was going to do it anyway.

I didn't waste any time; I went back to the dojo the next night to enroll. Monthly dues were five dollars (payable in advance), and my first uniform cost four dollars. It was nothing like the sharp cotton canvas uniforms of today, or even the thinner student gi. It was a thin, yellow-brown material which got increasingly whiter – and increasingly smaller – every time you washed it. Before long it was bright white and came down to just past my knees!

On my first night the dojo was crowded with (mostly) Okinawan students. They looked like supermen as I watched them warm up. One student was kicking the bottom of a heavy bag as big as me with his bare toes. With each kick the bag went flying a foot or two in the air. When he left the bag, eager to fit in, I went over to it and started punching. Understand, at this point I had absolutely no training, and the bag barely budged. But I kept at it; I made no impression on the bag (or the other students, some of whom were watching me with amusement), but I did manage to beat my hands red and sore. Progress!

Other students were stretching – to my untrained eye, almost to the breaking point – or punching a hard, wooden post, which would make that distinctive "clacking" sound with every strike. I couldn't imagine how they could keep punching those posts with their bare fists, over and over, without breaking a knuckle. I decided to take a safer (and less painful) course and imitate the stretchers. The intensity and dedication I saw all around me was amazing. And the sensei wasn't even in the room yet!

"Welcome to our world, Gaijin!"

Then Sensei Nagamine entered the room, and all activity and conversation came to an abrupt halt as students scrambled to assume their proper places. As I watched them scramble I realized I had no idea where to go or what to do. They lined up in neat, orderly rows, and one student after another directed me further and further to the back. Finally, I was on the far left in the back row, evidently where I belonged.

I followed the examples of those in front of me; when they knelt, I knelt; when they bowed, I bowed; when they sat back into *"seiza"* (kneeling, sitting on one's feet), I sat back into *seiza*. I grasped that it was a meditation period, I knew I was supposed to shut my eyes, but I didn't know when to open them. So I snuck peeks, hoping I wouldn't get caught. Then, in unison, we bowed from our kneeling positions, foreheads to the floor, and I was astonished to see Nagamine Sensei bow back to us. Then it was time to work out.

I had not yet been taught the proper stances or techniques, so I did my best to imitate those in front of me as we did hundreds of repetitions of basic punches, blocks and kicks. I was athletic; I played football in high school, and I thought Coach put us through some serious drills… but it was nothing compared to that night's workout. I was dripping with sweat and didn't think I had a drop left in the tank, when suddenly Sensei shouted "*Yame!*" and everyone ran back to their original positions. More kneeling, more bowing, and class was dismissed. Could I go through all this again tomorrow night? Hell, yeah! I was stoked!

As I was leaving, I noticed a tall American come into the dojo. I was surprised, because there were few Americans studying karate at the time, and doubly surprised because all the students seemed to be deferring to him and treating him with utmost respect. He was tall and well-muscled, with close-cropped blond hair. I pegged him as a Green Beret or Special Forces. I wanted to meet him, but I didn't get a chance; he was there for the black belt class that followed the under-belts. However, it did clear up one thing: my buddies at the base were wrong; an American could advance and gain some respect.

An important note here: it was very possible to create just the conditions my buddies suggested. If you left your ego at the door and came in with humility you could be accepted; if you walked in acting like you were superior because you were an American serviceman, you would pay. I remember the time a couple of swaggering G.I.s came into the dojo, walked up to the sensei, and demanded to be taught "k'roddy." The sensei smiled, said a few words to the senior student, and sat back to watch. The Americans were shown some strikes and kicks, a few blocks, and told to sit down. Then a pair of students stood up to spar.

A few seconds later the students sat down and the sensei told the Americans, "Your turn now." The G.I.s wanted to impress and they hit hard, but the sensei and the senior students kept shouting, "Harder!

Faster! C'mon, hit like men!" No matter how hard they fought, they were always urged "No! You want to learn karate! You have to hit harder!" "Block faster!" If one retreated to a corner, there was always a senior student there to push him back.

After a full minute they quit, dripping with sweat, limping, covered with bruises. After they left, the class and the teacher broke out in laughter.

"Did you see how hard he hit him? I thought he would break his ribs. Hahaha!"

"I thought that one time the guy was going to vomit all over the floor! Hahaha!"

"I'm sure he broke his toes with that kick! Hahaha!"

They took bets among themselves on whether the G.I.s would return. They never did.

No, arrogance is never good when dealing with Okinawans. Approach with humility and you will earn respect.

Any town with a military base has its districts notorious for drinking and nightlife, and they're usually worth staying away from. But young, testosterone-charged soldiers tend to lack that wisdom. In that part of Okinawa, it was a town called Namanui, with a long strip of bars and bar girls. I had been in Okinawa about a month, and I was spending more time in Namanui than I probably should have.

One night I was sitting in a bar with some buddies, hoisting a few drinks and listening to music, when a bunch of Navy guys came in and started to raise hell. For the record, they were submariners, recognizable for their beards. Only sub crews wore beards. It was probably a long-awaited shore leave, because these guys were laughing loudly, acting obnoxious, and spending furiously, buying drinks for all the bar girls. Suddenly, one of the guys stood up and started shouting at "his" girl; he found out she was drinking Cokes while he was paying for whiskey. They were standing face to face yelling at each other, when all of a sudden the guy dumped his beer on her. First mistake.

Kinjo, the Okinawan bouncer, stood about five foot two. Everyone liked Kinjo; he always wore a three-piece suit and a smile. Never losing his smile, Kinjo came over and started talking to the guy, but he was too far gone to listen to reason. Also, he was about six-two and pretty much used to getting his way. So now he turned from the girl and started getting directly in Kinjo's face, crowding him and abusing him verbally. Second mistake. Even for a nice guy like Kinjo, this was too much. The Okinawan bouncer asked him if he wanted to finish it outside, and the guy said "Let's do it!" Third (and final) mistake.

Kinjo and the sailor went outside and the crowd followed. First thing you saw was the sailor taking a swing. Next thing you saw was the sailor lying in the gutter, half-conscious, and his face covered with blood. Kinjo straightened his tie and strolled casually back into the bar like nothing had happened. The guy's buddies hustled him into a cab and took off for their base.

Eventually I became good friends with Kinjo, because I (almost) always behaved myself in his bar and (almost) never cause trouble. It turns out that Kinjo was a black belt studying *Gōjū-ryū* karate under Yagi Meitoku, whose dojo was near Namanui. I thought about asking Sensei Yagi for admission (you did not just walk into a dojo and slap down your money in Okinawa, you requested, humbly, to be accepted. There was no guarantee you would be). But it never happened.

Soon the Vietnam conflict heated up and my work day went from a normal nine to five to working twelve hour days, sometimes seven days a week. I could no longer train the way I had been training. Before long I had to give up my training at Sensei Nagamine's dojo. But I will always be indebted to him for introducing me to the true way of traditional Okinawan Karate. It is a debt I can never repay.

HOW I MET MY WIFE

It's time to backtrack a little, because the greatest influence in my Okinawan karate journey has to be my wife and her family. This is how we met:

After our first visit to Sensei Nagamine's dojo, my friend Tom and I decided to get something to eat before heading back to base. We were searching Naha Ichiba, the local marketplace, looking for "A-signs," an indicator that the establishment had passed health inspections and held to American safety and hygiene standards. We had been warned that afternoon to avoid restaurants that lacked the A-sign because of health risks but there was not an A-sign restaurant to be found. There were, however, two beautiful Okinawan girls standing and talking. They were obviously much higher class than the Namanui bar girls and almost seemed out of place. We decided these girls would know where there was a decent place to eat.

In Okinawa (as in anyplace else), it's considered bad form to just walk up to women you don't know, and these girls looked decidedly uncomfortable as we tried to convey what we wanted. They spoke no English and we spoke no Japanese but, with the aid of some creative pantomiming, we communicated what we needed, and the girls indicated that they understood. They had us follow them through the maze of the marketplace to a small restaurant we probably would never have noticed. It had no A-sign, but you know how readily a serviceman will trust a pretty girl, so we went in. The hostess spoke a little English (hallelujah!) and when the girls said "Sayonara!" we asked the hostess for help. We weren't about to let a pair of beauties like these off the hook that quickly! The hostess acted as intermediary as they agreed to meet us at the same restaurant the next night. It was an encounter that would change and define the rest of my life!

Before long, Tom decided he wanted to keep clubbing, but I was getting more and more infatuated with Miko, "my" girl. I'd see her every chance I got, and I even invested in a Japanese/English dictionary to help communicate. Miko seemed to like me as much as I liked her; even though we didn't understand each other's language, we would laugh and make fun of our communication challenges whenever we got together. I could not get her off my mind.

The author and Kiyoko Miko Teller at Namanui Beach in 1966

A month after arriving in Okinawa I bought a tiny, two-cylinder Mazda that struggled to get over hills – kind of a problem because Okinawa is *all* hills. But it was a car; it did give me some mobility, and I was able to explore the island. Miko always came along. The first road trip we took, she wanted to take me to a place called Suicide Cliff. I was a little apprehensive. It was the site of a bitterly fought battle during the recent World War where the Americans had pushed the Japanese to the far south of the island. The Okinawans had been told stories by the Japanese military of American cruelty to their captives and thousands chose suicide over capture. Many soldiers also found themselves caught between an overwhelming fighting force and a deadly cliff; they chose the cliff. Now there were exquisite monuments to the brave Japanese soldiers and Okinawans who chose death over surrender, but why would Miko take me there?

The author's first car a little two cylinder Mazda.

When we got to the top of the cliff, I found out. She leaned over and gave me my first kiss – a kiss I'll never forget! Then we walked around and looked at the monuments, Miko telling me what they represented. I felt distinctly out of place. There were a number of Japanese tourists there as well, and I couldn't shake the feeling that they were looking at me with distrust and resentment; it had been less than twenty years since the end of the war and many lost family and friends when the U.S. invaded Okinawa. Mixed with the soaring feeling of that kiss were strong feelings that I didn't belong there, where many Okinawans came to mourn their dead.

The author and Miko's first date, walking up to suicide cliff.

I had been in Okinawa about a year, and Miko and I were spending more and more time together. Finally, I got my courage up and decided to make it official – I asked her to marry me. She said she had been waiting for me to ask – hoping I would, in fact – but getting married in Okinawa is a lot more complicated than getting married in the States. First there was the dreaded ritual of meeting her family. We arrived at her home in Agena and, before entering, I took off my shoes as is the custom. Then, when I looked up to enter the house, her mother was standing right in front of me; although she was a head shorter she was looking right in my eyes. I don't know that I've ever been more frightened in my life! I thought I was facing the *Yama Uba*, a mythological Japanese witch!

Then, much to my surprise, Mama-san spoke to me in English. Was I happy? Did I like her daughter? What were my plans? In all, she was a charming woman. Papa-san, however, was a little less welcoming. I could see him in the next room, and he refused to come in and speak with me. I had no problem with that; he was quite big by Okinawan standards and looked at me with a scowl. Eventually he thawed a little – we even became friends – but that first meeting was not the best.

We were virtually married almost immediately, but the official process took almost a year. First, all Miko's family paperwork had to be translated into English by an official, a government-certified translator, a process known as *"apostilling."* When the documents were apostilled, I learned a surprising fact based on an Okinawan custom, carried over from Okinawa's previous association with China: rather than two years my senior, as I had thought, Miko was actually a year my junior. When an Okinawan baby is born, the time spent in the womb is taken into account. Therefore, at birth a baby is considered a year old. Then another year is added to the child's age every Chinese New Year. Thus, by American accounting, Miko was actually 2-1/2 years younger than her Okinawan age.

I learned another, even more surprising fact as well: Miko's name was not Miko, it was Kiyoko! When we first met she was afraid her parents would find out she was dating an American, so instead of her name she gave me an alias. I was so accustomed to calling her Miko that I continued to do so – and continue to do so to this day. Not many people outside her family realize that "Miko" is a phony name she made up on the spur of the moment more than fifty years ago. We were finally married on July 29, 1967.

OFF TO VIETNAM

My first tour of duty in Okinawa eventually ended and I was reassigned to the Cam Ranh Bay Air Base in Viet Nam. Miko and my oldest child Tina stayed behind in Okinawa, living with her mother until my return.

Cousin Jim Bunting and the author in Chu Lai, Vietnam 1968.

Cam Ranh Bay was supposed to be the safest place in Viet Nam; President Johnson had been there shortly before my arrival. However, the Tet Offensive was in full swing and there was really no safe place in the country, as I found out my very first night. That's when, just about midnight, the enemy hit our fuel dumps, lighting the place up like it was broad daylight and generating an incredible amount of heat. There were protocols, of course, but we hadn't been briefed yet. All the guys who had just arrived, including me, had no idea what to do; we didn't even know our way around the base. We were running around like so many squirrels on a busy highway. Once we weathered that first attack we were no longer considered newbies; we had graduated with honors!

We lived in hooches on the north side of the main base. There were only around fifty Air Force assigned to Cam Ranh Bay, the rest were all Army. To get to the main base, we had to take a truck. One evening we were bored and decided to go to the main base to watch the movie they always showed there in an open field. That night it was an episode of the TV show, *Combat*. We're sitting in the middle of a field, watching combat action, hearing and seeing actual gunfire in the distance. Planes were flying overhead, dropping flares that lit up the sky and engaging with the enemy. Now that's the way to watch combat; you can't get more realistic than that!

Another night we didn't need our own truck, we caught a ride with some Green Berets. They asked us where we were off to, and we told them we were going to the other side. They said, "That's where we're going, hop in the back." The ride to the other side of the base normally took about ten minutes, but we weren't paying attention; we were joking and laughing, and suddenly we realized we were in that truck a hell of a lot longer than that. We shouted to them, "Where are you guys going? This isn't the way to the main base!" They responded, "You said 'the other side'. We're going to the other side of the river."

They stopped the truck and told us, "We can't drive you back; you'll have to get out here and go back on foot." They were laughing. "Go straight back the way we came," they said, "but you'd better stay low to the ground. It's getting dark and who knows what's out there?" They were still laughing as they pulled away. To make things worse, the sky opened up like it only can in that part of the world and the rain was coming down in buckets. So we never saw combat... but we came pretty damn close!

My assignment in Cam Ranh Bay was flying on the C-130 cargo planes, loading and unloading pallets and flying on flare missions. It was an easy, relatively low-risk job, and although it seemed like a lifetime while I was there, the time passed pretty quickly.

Once that tour was completed, I returned to the States and was assigned to McGuire Air Force Base to complete my enlistment. My wife and daughter joined me there. It was Miko's first time in the United States, and every experience was new. After the quiet pace of Okinawa, Miko was astonished at how fast everything in the United States moved. But

February 15, 1968 Tet Offensive; The author's C-130 cargo plane in Khe Sahn delivering cargo under fire.

for me, life at McGuire was routine; almost a vacation after Viet Nam, and the time flew by. Before I knew it my enlistment was up; the Air Force wanted me to re-up, and I agreed on the condition that I would be assigned to Okinawa. So June of 1970 saw us all back in Okinawa: Miko and me, four-year-old Tina, and our newest addition, baby Jimmy, born about a year earlier. And that's when my life in karate really began.

2
HOHAN SOKEN AND FUSEI KISE

When we first arrived back in Okinawa, we stayed with Miko's parents in Agena while we waited for off-base housing. I mentioned that I'd like to get back into karate and Miko's mom told me she could help; her best friend's husband taught the art and had a dojo. Coincidentally, he was also my father-in-law's long-time friend. That's when I met Sensei Seikichi Odo.

Odo Sensei was small in stature but a huge figure in Okinawan martial arts. He studied karate under Shigeru Nakamura and kobudo under Shinpo Matayoshi. Odo Sensei worked at the army base, and that's where he taught most of his classes. Since his students at the time were mainly American servicemen, his tuition was significantly higher than many Okinawan dojos.

I was supporting a family of four on an Air Force salary, and I didn't think I could justify spending that much on my training. So I reluctantly looked for another place to train. Luckily, my wife's mother had another relative who studied karate, a nephew who studied with a gentleman named Fusei Kise.

I remember the drive to Sensei Kise's dojo for the first time. I was riding with my mother-in-law and her nephew, who spoke no English. She and her nephew were engaged in a conversation in Japanese, and then she turned to me and said, "Sensei Kise's style has techniques that make it easy to break bones, and he teaches secret killing techniques." She had obviously misunderstood much of what her nephew had told her, but I believed every word of it. Psyched? Hell, yeah! When we arrived and I met Sensei, my enthusiasm got the better of my manners and I blurted out, "I really want to learn how to break bones… and your secret killing techniques!" The look on his face was priceless. He looked at me, then he looked at my mother-in-law, then he looked back at me and broke into a big smile (testament to his sense of humor) and said, "Okay, Killer, let's get started!"

My father-in-law's first formal teacher was a gentleman named Tatsuo Shimabuku. His good friend Seikichi Odo was a student of Shimabuku as well. This was well before named "styles" came about; a student of Shimabuku was merely a student of Shimabuku. Eventually, Master Shimabuku's system became known as *Isshin-Ryū*, currently one of the world's foremost styles, but when my father-in-law trained with him it was merely the karate that Master Shimabuku taught.

Master Tatsuo Shimabuku

Okinawa was a different place after the war. Many traditions gave way to more modern ideas, including the tradition of keeping karate secret. No longer was it passed on only through family; changing times and economic realities opened it up to a wider audience. The largely agricultural economy gave way to a more cosmopolitan, retail environment, largely due to the immense population of G.I.s. Families that were traditionally farmers and craftsmen gave way to shopkeepers and tradesmen.

Karate schools began to spring up all over the island. Before long a number of American servicemen joined various dojos – the ones that would accept them. Many would not. Initially there was strong resentment for the Americans among the Okinawan students, and it did not die off easily – in fact, it has not completely disappeared to this day. Slowly over time as the Okinawan students trained and worked side by side with the *"gaijins,"* the resentments began to subside and hard work was respected. By the time I started my training, American students were widely accepted in most dojos.

One Sunday morning, after I had been studying under Sensei Kise for some time, I awoke to the sound of tools in the yard. My wife said it was a surprise; her father was making me my very own makiwara board. I ran outside to see the progress, and he told me that yes, it was my makiwara board, and no, I was not to touch it for 24 hours to allow it to cure. He said that the next day I could start training with it, and he would teach me the proper way to do so. Then he took a load of iron pipe and

The author striking his makiwara board.

cobbled together a sturdy rack to hang a heavy bag from. Next, he sent me inside to fetch my military duffle bag and instructed me to follow him. Together we drove to the beach, me thinking "what the hell?"

every step of the way, but the purpose of the bag dawned on me while we were filling it with sand. It would be my heavy bag! I practiced kicking that bag incessantly and it worked perfectly; after a short time, I could make it jump with every kick. Then the rain began. I don't know if you have ever kicked a bag filled with 100 pounds of wet sand, but it is not fun. I don't think concrete could have been heavier or more unyielding.

The night after he made me the makiwara board, my father-in-law took me outside and showed me how to strike it. He had affixed a section of an old tire near the bottom of the board and taught me how to kick it repeatedly to toughen up my toes. Looking back, I believe the makiwara board and kicking bag were not so much gifts, but tests. He wanted to see what kind of karate-ka I would be. At any rate, that's about when the tensions began to subside and a genuine friendship developed. My wife's parents became my second parents, and I learned a great deal from them besides karate. I am in awe of my father and mother-in-law's wisdom, and I can never repay them for all they gave me.

My wife, Miko, had been studying traditional Okinawan dance since she was four years old, and she was very accomplished. She danced professionally at tea houses, birthday celebrations, weddings, and many other functions. I had just been promoted to green belt when she surprised me with, "I'd like to study karate too. It is something we can do together and it will be fun."

"Are you sure?" I asked.

"Yes, my dance teacher always told us we should study karate. My dancing is filled with hidden karate movements. I think it would help me with my dancing."

So we started training together. And Miko was amazing! The first time she tested she was the only Okinawan woman in the group. There were a few American women testing, but they were all larger and more experienced than Miko. The testing group went through their warm-ups and basics, and then I was surprised to hear Sensei say, "Everyone who's testing, line up for bogu kumite."

Bogu kumite is a particularly vicious form of full-contact sparring. Competitors would don bamboo-and-leather armor similar to samurai armor, and fight full force. There was no holding back. Even worse, no one was matched for size, you fought whoever was next to you in line.

"In a real fight," Sensei Kise used to remind us, "You can't pick your opponent. You fight who you fight, and make the best of it." My little Miko was matched against an American female Air Force security policewoman who must have outweighed her by twenty-five pounds! There was my little wife, face to face with a seeming giantess. At each corner of the homemade ring stood a black belt to make sure the competitors stayed in the ring, and the center judge was Sensei Kise's senior black belt, a gentleman with a reputation for toughness. Then came the call to fight, *"Hajime!"*

I was astonished how fast my Miko was. No matter how hard and suddenly her opponent attacked, she was untouchable. All the Okinawan students were shouting encouragement, but Miko didn't need it; she was fearless! Sensei Kise was sitting in the corner laughing his ass off; he had no doubt Miko would prevail. The fight seemed to last forever, but when the dust settled Miko emerged victorious. And untouched. I remember thinking as we left the dojo that night, "I'm gonna have to train way harder. Miko can kick my butt anytime she wants!"

It was at one of sensei Kise's morning classes at the base when I first set eyes on Master Hohan Soken. He had silver-grey hair and a perfect military bearing. He was over eighty years old at the time, but walked and moved with the confidence and alertness of a man half his age. He didn't say much, but when he did talk Master Soken was soft-spoken and quiet. I remember thinking, "This is what a real karate master is like." He would frequently walk through our classes and give little pointers or corrections to the students.

One morning when the class was taking a break, Master Soken grabbed my wrist (I was still a white belt) and said something to Sensei Kise. Sensei Kisei said, "He wants you to block his punch." Then Master Soken struck me in the face (not gently); I had absolutely no way of blocking it. Then he told me (through Sensei Kise) to grab his wrist and punch him in the same manner. I went to punch him, confident that I could make contact, and he somehow trapped both my arms and hit me in the face again. He had an amused smile on his face. I asked him how he did it, and, with a chuckle, he replied (in Japanese), "Just keep practicing." Remember, I was a reasonably athletic twenty-something, and the man was in his eighties.

By the time I made brown belt, Sensei Kise had started teaching at other military bases around the island. Since he could not be at all the classes simultaneously, he placed one of his American black belts in charge of each of the dojos. The black belt would run the classes, and Sensei Kise would visit each week to supervise the instruction. However, the demand outpaced his promotions, and he eventually ran out of black belts. That's when he asked me to teach one of the classes.

"But Sensei, I'm only a brown belt. I'm not qualified to teach."

Robert Teller ikkyu (first kyu brown belt)

"Do you think you know better than I do who should be teaching my classes?" Ahem... I was starting to get nervous.

"Of course not, Sensei. But will they take instructions from a brown belt?"

"Americans still think black belt means expert. As a brown belt, you're the next thing to an expert. And you are a very good brown belt. Besides, I'll be visiting often."

So against my better judgement, I started teaching classes at Camp McTureous Marine Base in Agena. I taught three classes per week, and Sensei Kise usually managed to come by at least once a week. One-night Sensei Kise showed up with Master Soken in tow.

One of my students was a Marine Gunnery Sergeant who stood about six foot two and was built like a tank. He also had previous training in judo. That was too much for Master Soken; he told Sensei Kise to have the marine perform a judo technique on him. Remember, he was about five foot two and eighty-two years old. The gunny refused.

"I know he's a famous karate master and all, but look at him! He's a tiny, frail old man. I'm not gonna throw him!" the Gunny exclaimed.

Sensei Kise told Master Soken what he had said.

"Okay, have him grab me as though he's going to throw me." "I'll grab him but I'm not going to throw him." Sensei Kise just smiled.

Robert Teller receives first place for full contact bogu kumite from Master Hohan Soken.

"Yes, Master Soken and I both know that."

So the Gunny reached to grab Master Soken around the collar, and with unbelievable speed, Master Soken's hands tapped his much larger, younger, stronger opponent on the chest. Master Soken applied increasing pressure with only his fingers, and the Marine went down to his knees. "Try to move."

The gunny tried but was utterly unable to. Even Sensei Kise seemed amazed. I later asked the Marine how it felt and he replied, "It was really strange. It didn't really hurt and there wasn't that much pressure, but I just could not move! How did that old man do that?"

I gave him a look that suggested that I knew the trick, but of course I was as mystified as he was.

At age eighty-one, Master Soken, of course, was old-school; his Okinawa was not the modern Okinawa. In earlier times Okinawan folk dancing and karate were closely interrelated, and Maser Soken took great interest in showing Miko karate moves that were hidden in her dance. Meanwhile, she continued to practice her karate and was soon awarded her black belt by Master Soken and Sensei Kise.

In July of 1971, my son Scott Glenn came into the world. His middle name was in honor of Astronaut John Glenn. With three children to take care of – including an infant – Miko needed to take a break from her karate training. That did not affect her friendship with Master Soken however, and many mornings Master Soken and Sensei Kise would stop by our house on their way home from the dojo. Miko would make them lunch and they would sit and talk like old friends, usually about her Okinawan folk dancing. During these talks Master Soken would continue to demonstrate parallels between her dance and karate.

One morning Miko was in the yard hanging clothes on the line and little Jimmy was playing on his tricycle, when old "Sake Joe" and his younger cohort showed up. The two were alcoholics; no one knew where they lived, only that they would appear occasionally to beg money from the other soldiers' wives to buy alcohol.

Miko shouted to the other housewives, telling them, "Don't give them any money – they'll only keep coming back!"

One of the other wives responded, "I know. They come around almost every day."

Miko has been described many ways, but bashful is not among them. She shouted at the men in Japanese to go away and stop bothering the neighborhood women. The pair responded by starting toward my wife, threatening to hurt or kill little Jimmy. Miko might have earned a black belt from Okinawa's most respected karate master, but these were two drunk, full-grown men; even if she could overpower them both, one could engage her while the other snatched our boy. Miko grabbed Jimmy and Scott, who was in a stroller outside and ran into the house.

But Sake Joe and his friend would not go away; they started pounding on the door yelling threats. Miko tried to call me but I wasn't near a phone, and the men were still outside threatening. They finally gave up and left. That's when Master Soken and Sensei Kise arrived for their morning visit. They came in, still wearing their karate gis from the morning karate class, Soken with his red belt and Kise with his red-and-white, and found Miko sitting at the table crying. They asked her what happened, and she recounted the morning's incident with the two drunks. Just as she was finishing her story, guess who returned?

Master Soken was at the door even faster than the much younger Kise, and when Sake Joe saw Master Soken in front of him he fell to his knees begging for mercy. His younger friend, however, took off running. Sensei Kise wanted to kill Sake Joe, and easily could have (remember his "secret killing techniques"?). Under the circumstances he would not even have been prosecuted!

Master Soken interceded. "Let me talk to him. If that doesn't change his attitude, *then* you can kill him."

Master Soken put his hand on Joe's shoulder and began talking to him in the old Okinawan dialect, *Uchinaaguchi*. He spoke at length, and very softly. When he was finished speaking, Sake Joe was crying. Soken told my wife to fix Joe some Okinawan tea. They talked awhile longer, the old karate master and the old drunk, and then the man got up to leave. Miko said he was bowing all the way out the door.

"You won't see them again," said Master Soken.

And she didn't.

During one of their "breakfast clubs." Master Soken casually mentioned that he had been asked to demonstrate Okinawan folk dance on Armed Forces Television.

"That's wonderful", said Miko. "That will be a great show!"

"You don't understand," said Master Soken. "I want you to come demonstrate with me. More and more Americans are taking karate classes, and I want to show the relationship between the dances and martial arts. Nobody combines both as skillfully as you do."

Miko could hardly believe her ears – but with a pitch like that, how could she refuse? The demonstration was a brilliant success; I'm only sorry that in the early seventies they did not routinely record every show. I'd give anything to have a copy of it.

One day after our morning class, a number of us were standing around talking about karate and martial arts, and the subject of Isshin-Ryū karate came up. I think someone had heard of it and was asking how it differed from our style.

My ears perked up. "My father-in-law studied with Tatsuo Shimabuku before his art was ever called Isshin-Ryū!"

Now it was Sensei Kise's turn to be surprised. "Your wife's father studied karate?"

"I'd better not say any more," I said.

"No, no, no!" said Sensei Kise. "Tell me more. Or even better, bring your father-in-law to class."

Robert Teller training with Master Fusei Kise.

"I'll do my best." I said, but I knew he wouldn't come.

When next I saw my wife's parents I asked my father-in-law to stop by our class.

"Sensei Kise would like to meet you."

"What does he want to talk about?"

"Oh, I don't know. He likes to meet people. Maybe karate in the old days?"

My father-in-law didn't respond, but he didn't go. The next day I went to class and Sensei Kise asked where my father-in-law was.

"Didn't you give him my invitation? Didn't you tell him I want to meet him?" Sensei Kise was not happy.

"You don't understand, Sensei. My father-in-law is a very quiet person. He's reserved. He likes to stay home. And he doesn't like for people to know he had practiced karate."

"Okay," said Sensei, "If he won't come meet me, I'll go meet him."

So after class, Sensei Kise, still in his karate gi, jumped into my car and off we went to Agena to meet my father-in-law.

We knocked on the door, and when my father-in-law opened it and saw Sensei Kise, in his karate gi, standing in the doorway, his jaw dropped to the floor. It was so amusing I started to laugh, only to be met with an ugly scowl from my father-in-law. I did my best to hide my amusement. It's never the best idea to piss off one's father-in-law!

My father-in-law kept saying to Sensei Kise, "Come in! Come in and sit down! Please... come in!" (In Japanese, of course).

Sensei Kise, smiling, took a step into the house and my father-in-law showed him to a seat, while my mother-in-law fixed a batch of her finest tea. The two older men started talking; the talk got more and more animated and within a few minutes, although they had never met before, they were yammering and laughing like old, long-lost friends. They talked for almost an hour. When I dropped Sensei Kise off at his house, he told me he really liked my father, that he was a true, old-school karate man. Then he really surprised me. He said he invited him to our next testing, and he wanted him to sit by his side on the testing board. Those of my readers familiar with Okinawan karate protocol understand what an honor that was. I couldn't wait to go home and tell Miko!

It was on a Thursday or Friday, after our morning workout, that Sensei Kise asked for volunteers. He said that Master Soken's grandson was getting married, and would any of us would like to volunteer for a couple of days to help build a house. The house would be on Master Soken's property; his friend would be building it but the carpenter would need help with manual labor, like unloading blocks and bricks from the truck and hauling them to where they needed to be. Of course, all three of the lower-level belts volunteered eagerly. A chance for face time with Hohan Soken!

The following morning after class, the three of us piled into Sensei Kise's car and headed out on the half-hour drive to Master Soken's home in Gaja Village, Nishihara City. Time to rest? Hell no! As soon as we arrived we were put right to work, unloading cement blocks by the truckload and performing other manual labor. The work we did was hard, hot, sweaty and anything but glamourous. Noon, however, was lunch break, and we would sit around the table enjoying the delicious Okinawan food Master Soken's wife lovingly prepared for us. I'll never forget her amazing miso soup. After lunch the others would sit and talk for a while, but I felt more like walking so one day while they talked, I wandered around the grounds.

Master Soken had a small dojo on his property, and I noticed some unusual items piled outside. I thought they might be anchors for some type of construction. They were concrete blocks about the size of a number ten coffee can, and each had an iron pipe protruding from the middle. Master Soken noticed that I was taking an interest in them, so he came over. He neither spoke nor understood much English, but I managed to ask him what the odd concrete blocks were for. He laughed, and, grabbing one by the very end of the protruding pipe, he turned the device so the block was on top. Then, using only the strength of his wrist, he slowly lowered it until it was perpendicular to the ground. Then he brought it into his chest, and worked it in and out, in and out, to and from his chest. At age eighty-one, he made it look easy. Pretty soon everyone stopped talking and came over to watch.

"Why don't you try it?" asked Sensei Kise.

"Sure, no problem!"

After all, I had just watched a skinny old man fling this thing around like a feather. I picked it up, pointed the block at the sky, and proceeded to imitate Master Soken. It didn't work out quite as planned. As I began to lower the block, I realized I couldn't control the weight and I almost dropped it on my foot. The only thing that quelled the laughter was that nobody else had any more success with it than I did. Master Soken suggested I keep trying, and walked away. So every day I rushed through my lunch and hurried to the little dojo to work on my coffee can. The last day we were there, Master Soken told Sensei Kise I could keep the homemade training device. He had several, and mine was the smallest one! He said I should work with it every day until I could do ten reps with each hand. So I diligently worked with that block every day, and when I finally managed a single rep I screamed with joy! It took months, but eventually I got up to my ten reps on each side. I still work out with that same concrete coffee can I got from Master Soken, and at age seventy I can still crank out my ten reps.

Sensei Kise's senior student at the Kadena Air Base dojo was Tomo Kuda, in his mid-twenties and the son of an overall senior student, Yuichi Kuda. Under Sensei Kise's direction, the younger Kuda led the classes at the base. After lining up and bowing in, we'd head out to the large concrete slab outside the rec center and do our "*jumbi undo*," or calisthenics, to warm up the "karate muscles." Then we'd stretch all the muscles we just warmed up.

After stretching, we'd move on to "*kote ate*," or body toughening. This drill is practiced in just about every Okinawan dojo, sometimes under the name "*kote kitae*." Then basics – punches, double punches, strikes, blocks, and a variety of kicking drills. After practicing all our basics, we'd take a short break before coming back for partner drills –

essentially repeating all the previous drills but with a partner, called "*yaku-soku kumite.*"

Then we moved on to Master Soken's personal form of *toide*, "*tai-sabaki*," or body-changing drills. These are essentially the art of executing subtle body shifting, with the effect of not being where your opponent is attacking. Then we worked on *kata*. Sensei Kise did not seem to emphasize kata the way Sensei Nagamine had. We'd practice kata in a group, performing each kata three or four times. When you had finished the highest-level kata you knew, you'd break off and continuing practicing all the kata you knew on your own.

Sensei Kise's training was unique, in that he mixed empty-hand kata with *kobudo* (weapons) kata. All the other sensei I knew of separated the two. After kata practice came the fun (and painful!) part: *bogu kumite*. We'd fight full contact for about a half-hour. If we had a special event coming up, such as testing or a tournament, we'd add the headgear and fight for half the class. Bogu kumite was always part of our testing regimen.

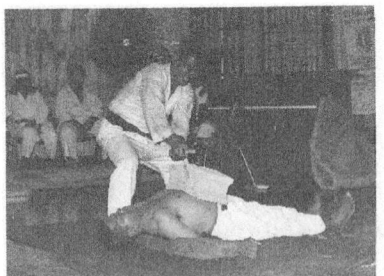

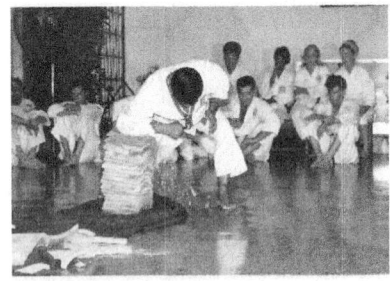

Sensei Kise doing demo at the Rec Center Kadena AB in the early 1970s.

During my time studying with Sensei Kise, it seems to me that his methods progressed through three distinct phases to arrive at his Kenshin-kan system as it is taught today. Initially Sensei Kise studied with Shuzen Maeshiro, a disciple of Chotoku Kyan's system of Shōrin-ryū. It was a hard, direct, bruising method known as Shōrinji-ryū; it entailed heavy kata training and lots of full-contact kumite. Classwork was harsh, intense, and sometimes brutal. All Sensei Kise's original Okinawan and American students studied Shōrinji-ryū.

Then Sensei Kise met and became a disciple of Hohan Soken. This was shortly before I arrived in Okinawa. Master Soken's karate was softer and more internal than Sensei Maeshiro's. When I first started training with Sensei Kise, the Shōrinji-ryū influence was still strong and workouts were still brutal and exhausting. But as time went on the karate started to become softer. I don't know if it was just me (remember, I was still essentially a novice), but through my karate career I had become used to hard, direct contact, and this new emphasis on softer techniques seemed weaker. The more Sensei Kise studied with Master Soken, the softer his karate seemed to become.

Strangely, whenever I visited Master Soken's dojo, I saw his three or four students practicing with full power! It was not what Sensei Kise was teaching at the base, and I was not happy. Meanwhile, Sensei Kise's karate "empire" was spreading. His classes at the base were getting crowded, and he

Makabe Sensei, Grandmaster Hohan Soken, and the author, Robert Teller.

was opening dojos at other bases as well. Then he started taking trips to the United States. The busier he became spreading his karate gospel, the less his students saw of him. He was spending so much time with his classes at military bases that his students at his own off-base dojo began to quit. Why study with a sensei you never saw? Eventually he actually closed his home dojo.

There were rumors that a rift was opening between Hohan Soken and Fusei Kise. Sensei Kise was teaching different kata and was not following Master Soken's methods. Sensei Kise's dojos on military bases were getting bigger and more widespread, and his American G.I.

students were returning to the States and opening dojos of their own. Sensei Kise opened a new home dojo off-base in Goya, Okinawa City, and named his new system Kenshin-kan. At only forty-one or forty-two years old, when most Okinawan karateka were still learning, Sensei Kise had established his own karate system!

I was teaching at a marine base, but I was receiving precious little instruction of my own and my frustration grew. I mentioned it to my wife's father, and he suggested it was time for me to find another teacher.

He said, "You need to look for a dojo that does not have American students. As long as you study at a dojo for Americans, you'll never learn true Okinawan karate."

"Maybe Master Soken will accept me as a student," I said.

"That wouldn't be very smart," replied my father-in-law. "Sensei Kise could feel insulted."

I eventually ended up studying with the amazing Shugoro Nagazato, but I didn't break with Sensei Kise immediately.

3
SHUGORO NAKAZATO

At that time, many American military bases in Okinawa were in transition and being returned to the Japanese. Naha was among them. All the military personnel stationed at the Naha base were transferring to Kadena and all that was left at Naha was base housing. I put my name on a waiting list for housing at Naha, even though the drive from Naha to Kadena was an hour or more. As a lower rank, I should have had a long wait, but apparently no one wanted to make the drive. It wasn't long before I was approved for housing at Naha. I still was not sure I wanted to move, but when Miko and I went to Naha to look, my reluctance disappeared. There were many homes available, and I qualified for a house much larger and more luxurious than my Kadena quarters. Plus, I never really minded long drives – in fact, I enjoyed them – so my family moved to Naha. This also gave me an excuse to break from Sensei Kise – but it was not to be... at least not immediately.

Sensei Kise told me to start a dojo at Naha; that Tomo Kuda lived near Naha and we could teach classes together. He promised me that he would visit the dojo at least once a week and bring Master Soken with him. This, of course, was before his break from Soken. The showing, however, was poor, and soon we were forced to admit defeat and cancel the classes.

I changed my work schedule to the midnight shift, which gave me my days free to train and go to classes, and had the added benefit of cutting down the traffic to near zero. During the day there was bumper-to-bumper traffic between Naha and Kadena. Changing to the midnight shift cut my drive time in half.

Along the way, in a little town near Naha called Aja, I noticed a huge billboard that read "KARATE." The more I passed the billboard, the more I wanted to find the school. So one day I took a side trip to

Aja to search for the dojo. I couldn't find it. It took me three trips to find it, tucked away in a little side alley too narrow for my car. It was closed, but the hours were posted on the door. I asked someone where the sensei lived, and he pointed to the apartment above the dojo. I knocked on the door but I got no response.

"Just as well," I thought. "I'll come back tomorrow with Miko. She can translate for me."

We returned the following day and knocked on the door, but again, no response. We knocked again. Finally, on the third knock, the most impressive man I ever saw opened the door. He wasn't that big or that imposing, but he looked at you with eyes that seemed to pierce right down to your soul. He did not smile, but he asked us in. That was my first encounter with Sensei Shugoro Nagazato.

Everything in his house was very formal, and everything had its place. He showed us to some chairs and we started to talk. I had asked Miko not to tell Sensei Nagazato that I had previously studied karate, because I wanted to start fresh as a white belt. I was talking while Miko translated, but Sensei Nagazato did not look at Miko even once; he kept that disconcerting gaze fixed on me – he didn't even blink! – and I got the feeling that even if he didn't speak English he knew exactly what I was saying – and a lot that I wasn't saying.

After about ten minutes, his wife came home, saw there were visitors, and ran to the kitchen for tea and cookies. The teacups were thimble-sized and she filled them only halfway, but she kept on pouring. Sensei Nagazato mentioned that his wife was a teacher of Okinawan dance, and I got the feeling he was very proud of that fact. I mentioned that my wife danced as well. That piqued his interest. His wife asked who her teacher was, and it turns out that she knew her. The fact that they had something in common seemed to break the ice.

Much of the rest of the evening was filled with a conversation in Japanese between Miko and Sensei Nakazato's wife, with Nakazato throwing in an occasional comment or question. Sometimes during these questions his eyes would shift to me, leaving me feeling markedly uncomfortable. He was not the smiling type! But finally, to my relief, I was told I was accepted as a student: classes met every day except Sunday, from one to three and six to nine. Wednesday's classes were reserved for kobudo.

After we had bowed our thanks and were getting ready to go home, Sensei Nakazato stopped my wife with a motion; there were things he wanted to explain. He did not want us to think he was stingy the way he served tea, but the tea represented life. In life, everything is meant to be done in moderation; never do anything to excess or extreme, and do not fill your cup so full there is no room for more. Drink what you are served, and more will always be forthcoming. I left the house with the impression I had finally met a true master, with as much wisdom as karate knowledge.

I never formally told Sensei Kise I was leaving. I wanted to sample Sensei Nakazato's training methods and assess the other students before I said my farewells. The first day's training with Sensei Nakazato had me so hyped that I never went back Sensei Kise's dojo again. If that was bad manners I apologize, but I was amazed with what I was seeing.

When I started, there was only one other American student, and he was a civilian. Sensei Nagazato told me he had once had many American students, but the U.S. Army had moved eighty percent of its personnel off Okinawa, and with the closing of Naha Air Base there weren't many Americans left near his dojo. I think he said it as a kind of an apology, but I didn't mind a bit! I wanted to train the way the Okinawan students trained.

Initially I went to both classes, and I was mesmerized by the way the students trained. Even at Master Soken's dojo with only Okinawan students, I had never seen kata performed with such blazing speed and raw power! These students were so far above me! I think I spent my first few sessions in a daze.

Initially I went to both afternoon and evening classes, and I was totally amazed by the students. I was as gung-ho as it gets to learn this new level of karate. I attended the afternoon classes when I could, but mostly I went to the evening classes. I was one of the few that was consistently there the full three hours. Everyone worked, and many of the Okinawans were taxi drivers, bus drivers, restaurant workers, and others, whose work schedule wouldn't allow them stay for the whole

The author Robert Teller with Grandmaster Shugoro Nakazato.

class. In fact, there were students coming and going all evening – the class that bowed out at the end of the night was never the same as the class that bowed in at six. Sensei Nakazato used to say that he didn't care if you only came for thirty minutes, as long as for that full thirty minutes you gave one hundred percent.

I usually arrived ten or fifteen minutes early, and by that time the dojo was normally filled with Okinawan teens, chasing, horsing around, and generally having a good time. At exactly six, Sensei Nakazato would enter the dojo, and all the horsing around came to an abrupt end. The kids – and the few adult students who were there at that hour – would snap into an attention stance, waiting for Sensei to come to the dojo floor. Then we'd quickly line up, kneel in "*seiza*" position and begin "*moksou*" (meditation). At a sharp command from a senior student, we'd then bow to Sensei Nakazato in front to the *shinza* (a small shrine established to honor the elders). Then Sensei would begin working with the kids.

To the consistent sounds of their moaning, he would line them up along he dojo perimeter and have them do "duck walks" until they fell over. This was ostensibly punishment for their earlier horseplay ...but they never seemed to learn! Every evening they would be roughhousing around the dojo before class, and every class would begin with their punishment! Sensei Nakazato loved his young students and they were in mortal fear of him!

Sensei Nakazato would start the adult students by warming up on *kihon* (basic) katas. Then he brought the kids up for *kihon*, and the adults would move to the back of the dojo for makiwara practice, individual warm-up exercises, or sparring. We used zero padding or safety equipment – no mouth guards, no groin cups, no hand- foot- or head-pads… no protection of any kind; just knuckles and toes against flesh. There was supposed to be no face contact, but, of course, "accidents" happened! Once you take a hard fist to the face or a kick to the groin, you learn to block and cover up any way you can.

The kids were usually out by about seven p.m., and the adult class started in earnest. Sensei Nakazato would call us up in groups, by belt color, and drill us on the katas we were on – our newest kata first, then down, in order, to your first kata. By the time you were finished drilling on kata your gi was usually wringing wet – and then you'd go to the back and spar while the next group drilled. Eventually he'd work through all the belt levels and it would start all over again. Sensei Nakazato would drill us on kata until we could hardly stand up – the sparring sessions in between served as rest periods! About a half-hour before the end of class he'd call up the highest level black belts; when your last kata came up you joined in, and you stayed in until all the katas (and students) were exhausted. Then we would perform a formal bow-out and Sensei Nakazato would leave the dojo and that's when the most intense training began! For about the next forty-five minutes the black belts would take over the class and the training was brutal. You'd usually leave with blood on your gi. I did not always stay for after-class class.

Learning a kata in Sensei Nakazato's dojo was quite an experience. In learning a new kata, I'm accustomed to having it broken down into manageable pieces and having it taught at half speed.

Sensei Nakazato correcting the author's kata.

I'm also used to asking questions to clarify certain points. In Sensei Nakazato's dojo it's a little bit different. There, when you learn a new kata, a black belt takes you to the back of the dojo and performs the full kata at full speed. No manageable pieces. No slowing it down. Your instructor does the kata, and you try to follow along – no questions permitted! Eventually, after many repetitions, the kata starts to make sense and the student picks it up, little by little. Without talking, without asking questions, the student is forced to figure everything out in his head.

THE HANDICAPPED STUDENT

I don't remember his name so I'll call him Oshiro. Oshiro was severely handicapped; he had a cleft palate and lip, and he couldn't walk well. Nevertheless, he was one of Sensei Nakazato's black belts and he came to almost every afternoon class. He couldn't come evenings because it conflicted with his job. Oshiro worked at night as a chef. I was still only a white belt, but we became friends. We would spar every afternoon; I usually won but it didn't matter – we were having fun.

One afternoon Oshiro was not there yet; it was just me and an Okinawan student – a school teacher who spoke English. Sensei Nakazato said a few words to the teacher, who turned to me and said Sensei Nakazato wanted to tell me about Oshiro; that he (the school teacher) would translate. Here is Oshiro's story:

As a little boy, unable to walk, Oshiro got around on a little roller board, somewhat similar to a mechanic's creeper. He would come to the dojo and surreptitiously watch through the window. Initially Sensei Nagazato ignored him, but after a while he decided to chat with him. When he approached, however, little Oshiro scooted away. It was more than a week before Oshiro returned to watch the class, and this time Sensei Nakazato decided to just leave him be; the boy was obviously fascinated with watching the classes and there was no point in scaring him away again.

Oshiro came to watch almost every day, and after a month or two Sensei Nakazato began to speak to him... not approach him, or even look at him, just speak to him. It took a while, but eventually little Oshiro would nod his head when Sensei spoke to him; he couldn't talk and it was an acknowledgement that he was hearing. After another month, Sensei asked Oshiro if he'd like some candy; the boy lit up with a smile and enthusiastically nodded his head yes. It was the beginning of a long and great friendship.

After another couple of months, Sensei Nakazato asked Oshiro if he wanted to learn karate, since he was obviously enjoying watching. Oshiro shook his head no and tried to show Sensei that he couldn't walk. Of course, Sensei knew that, but after a while he convinced him that he really could learn karate and persuaded him to try. Oshiro proved a very diligent student. He came to class every day, and after class Sensei Nakazato would work with him one on one for about forty-five minutes. In a matter of months Oshiro started to walk on his own. For most stories that alone would be a great ending, but in this one it was only the beginning!

Sensei Nakazato related that Oshiro gave his karate everything he had; even though progress was slow he worked himself into the ground. It took a couple of years, but he finally learned his first kata, and after about five years he was awarded his black belt. From constant training and interacting with his fellow students, Oshiro opened up and began to talk and communicate. One of Sensei's other afternoon students owned a restaurant, and offered Oshiro a job washing dishes. Although he had to learn even that simple task, he proved such an apt student that the restaurant owner began teaching him to cook. It wasn't long after that Oshiro became head cook and customers began commenting on how much better the food was.

I had known that Oshiro was somewhat handicapped, but I never knew to what degree, or how hard he had had to work to achieve all that he had achieved. I began to feel really guilty about sparring with Oshiro. Sensei Nakazato gave me a cryptic smile and sent me on my way.

ROBERT GETS A BEAT-DOWN

I tend to be rather light-hearted; I'm not exactly the class clown, but I'm easy-going. Not long after Sensei Nakazato told me about Oshiro, I was talking and joking with some other students while I was waiting to be called up for kata. I should have been sparring, but the fact is, although I really liked kata training, I wasn't that into kumite.

All of a sudden, I heard Sensei Nakazato talking with a black belt in a loud voice, and the black belt replying. They seemed to be in some sort of argument. The next thing I knew, the black belt had grabbed me by the gi and was dragging me to the back of the dojo. He shouted "*KUMITE!*" and before I was even finished bowing I saw his spinning back kick coming at me. I managed to get my foot up for a block, but it was to no avail; my opponent's kick was so powerful I went flying across the room and landed on my butt. I was still struggling to my feet when I felt the elbow land on the top of my head and saw stars. This guy wasn't playing around! He continued to batter me without mercy; I was almost unconscious when some other students rushed over and pulled him off me. My eyes were shut and I think my nose was broken, but I managed to glance over at Sensei Nakazato, who was still calmly calling kata as though nothing had happened.

When my kata was called I lined up in back and went through it as best I could, and then I quietly slipped out the door to my car. On the way to my car I remember telling myself that I was through – that I never wanted to see that dojo again and would not be returning. When

I walked into my house, as soon as my wife saw me she screamed and hustled me back into the car to the base hospital. I was treated and excused from duty that night. It took several days to recuperate -- days filled with deep soul-searching. I had come to Nakazato's dojo to learn real Okinawan karate. Now, after one bad beating, I wanted to quit? How could I face my wife's father? How could I face myself? No, I wouldn't quit, no matter what.

After four days of recovering, I returned to the dojo for afternoon class. Sensei Nakazato and the schoolteacher were already there, and they both looked at me as though I was a ghost. Then Sensei Nakazato smiled and asked how I was feeling. I replied that

Robert Teller working out in Master Nakazato's dojo.

I felt well enough to train. With the help of the schoolteacher, Nakazato said he never expected to see me again; it was he who instructed the black belt to beat me bloody. He didn't like my casual attitude; even if I was only there for a half hour he expected one hundred percent, and that fifty percent for three hours was not sufficient.

He also said he thought I was disrespecting Oshiro, who, he said, was twice the martial artist I would ever be. He also stated that he knew I was one of Kise's black belts, and felt disrespected on his own account because I never told him. I told him I didn't think it was important, and asked him how he knew. He replied that he knew from the beginning because of the "sissy" way I did kata. Then he imitated Kise's kata, while everyone laughed. I apologized profusely, bowed a thousand bows, and asked him if I would be permitted to continue training with him. I told him I would stop joking around and give a hundred percent every minute I was in the dojo. I promised he'd see a big difference.

He agreed to let me continue to train, and told me that the black belt who kicked my butt felt really bad about it. He said the guy initially said no, he didn't want to hurt me, but Sensei said that if he didn't do as instructed, he, Nakazato, would hurt him even worse. I was relieved and grateful to be permitted back. It was a while before I returned to evening class, but the first time I did the black belt who beat my ass came right over and apologized. We shook hands and became best of friends. As soon as I finished kata, he would grab me, drag me to the back (uh-oh!), and work with me on my sparring. After a while he would assign other black belts to spar with me, and if I wasn't holding my own he would be on me like white on rice. He was relentless… but I was finally learning. After some time he began bringing me to his house on Sundays to teach me to break wood and tiles – two skills we never worked on at the dojo. I don't remember his name, but I owe him everything! He taught me the true essence of Okinawan karate, and it is through him, as much as anyone, that Okinawan karate became my life.

One thing that intrigued me about Sensei Nakazato's dojo was that groups of students from the United States and around the world would make pilgrimages there. Senseis would take groups of students on tour to visit various dojos, and Sensei Nakazato's was always a highlight of the trip. It was not something he looked forward to; he hated the interruptions, but he would always pause the class and address the visitors politely for a few minutes. Then he would excuse himself and remark that he had to get back to his class.

PROMOTIONS IN SENSEI NAKAZATO'S DOJO

In most dojos in Okinawa and elsewhere, promotion day is a big deal. The promotion day was scheduled a week or more in advance; students knew the requirements for each belt level, and they spent days practicing their required techniques and kata. When testing day arrived, they bowed in as usual and then sat at the back of the dojo as individual students – or all the students testing for a particular rank – were called up and put through their paces. Once everyone who was eligible tests, they line up to bow out and the sensei called them by name, one by one, to hand them their certificate (and often their new belt). When everyone had their certificate, they bowed out and the class was over. It was often followed by a small party or celebration.

It was a little different in Nakazato's dojo. For kyu-level students (under black belt), there was no announced "promotion day." Sensei Nakazato had been monitoring every student every day, and knew exactly who had earned a promotion. He did not want the students to experience the stress of practicing specifically for a test. When he felt one or more students were ready to advance in rank, he wrote their certificates and stashed them behind the shinza. No one was aware they were going to be promoted. After the bowing-in ceremony but before class, he would retrieve the certificates, read them in Japanese, hand them out, and the students would scurry to put them away. The students would be responsible for obtaining their own belts, and promotion fees were due at the next class.

Testing at Master Nakazato's dojo.

At black belt level, students do test. It is expected that by the time they reach that grade they were able to control their stress and face testing in a calm, relaxed manner – just as they would have to do on the street. Proper breathing, proper focus, and control of one's emotions were necessary for advancement through black belt, as well as for success in actual fighting. Black belts test individually, with increasingly demanding physical requirements, from first to sixth dan. Promotion above sixth dan depends on what the student returned to the dojo and to karate in general. Teaching, acting as a good-will ambassador, developing new interpretations for kata, and many other factors came into play.

One day, when I showed up for afternoon class, who was sitting with Sensei but Tadashi Yamashita, a rising star in Hollywood martial arts films! Sensei told me I would test for my *shodan* (first level black belt) on Saturday, and told me what my requirements would be. Two other students, both Okinawan, were testing for their shodan as well. Then he told me Sensei Yamashita was also being promoted that day, from seventh degree to eighth degree.

When I arrived at the dojo for testing there was a small table set up; Sensei Nakazato, Sensei Yamashita, and two other high-ranking black belts were seated at it. Besides the testing board and the students to be tested, the dojo was pretty much empty – a relief because I did not want to test for my first black belt in front of a crowd. We did our initial warm-ups, went through some basics, and then performed our kata.

When we were finished, we lined up and Sensei Nakazato handed out our certificates. He also handed Sensei Yamashita his eighth-degree certificate and a new red-and-white belt. Promotions were over, and I was officially a black belt! As I turned to leave, Sensei Yamashita stopped me.

Tadashi Yamashita seated right of Sensei Nakazato.

"Where are you headed?"

"I'm going to Shureido (the local martial arts supply store) to pick up my black belt."

"What a coincidence! My mother lives near Shureido and I'd like to visit her. Can you give me a lift?"

Wow! One of the biggest karate film stars in Hollywood, and I'm giving him a lift to his mother's house! Sensei Yamashita speaks excellent English, probably due to all the time he's spent in Hollywood, and we talked all the way to Shureido. He told me his future film plans (which, unfortunately didn't really pan out). When we arrived at our destination, everyone knew him. We all talked and joked around, and when I went to pay the two dollars for my belt, I was informed that Sensei Yamashita had already paid for it. Wow again! Wait until I tell my wife that Tadashi Yamashita bought me my first black belt! We said our goodbyes, wished each other luck for our future plans, and parted ways. I never saw him again.

Shortly after earning my black belt, my enlistment period was coming to an end. I could either re-enlist and spend another four years in the Air Force or take my honorable discharge and become a civilian for the first time in ten years. It was not an easy decision. The Viet Nam war was coming to an end, and after a long, heart-to-heart talk with Miko, I decided to leave the service. I told Sensei Nakazato I was planning to return to Philadelphia, and he suggested I look up Bob Herten in New Jersey. Bob was one of his students who had been in Okinawa with the U.S. Army, and was now running a successful karate school in Patterson, N.J. I mentioned to Sensei that I, too, would like to open a school someday, and he surprised me by telling me that I'd make a very good teacher and if I wanted to open a school I had his blessing. I should talk to Bob Herten for some insights.

4
MY RETURN TO THE UNITED STATES

The author's family.

As the day approached for my return to the United States, I was getting increasingly nervous. I hadn't been a civilian for a decade, and I wasn't sure I remembered how. What kind of job could I get? Where would I live? The military was all I knew but I found a full-time job working with the Air Force Reserves in Atlantic City, New Jersey, and we rented a small townhouse in nearby Hammonton. Shortly after I settled in I got in touch with Bob Herten, who invited me to an upcoming seminar.

That Friday after work, my wife and kids and I drove up to Paterson and got a motel room near Bob's dojo. When I arrived at the seminar the next day, I found a virtual "Who's Who" of Sensei Nakazato's American Shorinkan students. Bob Herten, of course, but also in attendance were Noel Smith, Frank Hargrove, Sid Campbell, Ernest

Estrada and others. Bob went out of his way to make me feel welcome, but I was a little uncomfortable, mingling with all the Nakazato black belts. I believe they thought I had been a student of Sensei Nakazato for much longer than I actually had been; I had just received my black belt a few months before returning to the states, and they were all much more advanced than I was. But I still felt welcome and I really enjoyed the seminar.

On the way home from the seminar, I told Miko that I was really impressed with Bob Herten's dojo and the camaraderie of his students. I told her that's what I'd like my dojo to be like – a family, where everyone helped everyone else. I mentioned that there were no karate schools in Hammonton, so I could open a dojo right in our hometown. Plus, the pay at my regular job was not great, and a few extra dollars coming in from a karate school would be a big help. Miko agreed.

The next day I called Bob Herten and told him my thoughts.

"Bob.", he said, "I think that's a great idea. Go for it. I'll give you all the help I can."

He suggested starting out at a YMCA or an American Legion hall, where the rent and overhead would be minimal. Conveniently, there was an American Legion hall a few blocks from my house; I went there and told them I was recently discharged from the military and wanted to start a karate school. To my surprise, they were delighted and asked me how soon I could get started. They said I could teach Mondays, Wednesdays and Fridays, and for the first month rent would be free to help me get established.

I put small ads in all the local newspapers and saturated the town with flyers. Registration would be Monday, Wednesday and Friday from six to eight pm. I was hoping for an initial class of about ten students. Then, much to my surprise, we registered thirty students that first week! I was on Cloud Nine! At their first class, the students would pay their first month's tuition and the cost of their uniform.

I called Bob Herten and asked him where he got his uniforms, and he told me the name and address of a shop in New York City. He said the store closed at noon on Saturdays, and if I wanted the uniforms for my first Monday class, I'd have to drive up and pick them up on Saturday morning. Never having been to New York, I promptly got lost, but after wandering the New York streets for about an hour, I finally found the shop at about eleven forty-five, so, in the nick of time, I was able to get the needed uniforms. Now I needed a name for the school.

Bob Herten called his school the Okinawan Karate Institute, and whenever I called, his secretary answered "OKI – How can I help you?" I thought that sounded quite professional; I didn't want to plagiarize Bob Herten's name so I called my school the Okinawan Karate Academy. By a month or two in operation, the Okinawan Karate Academy had registered more than fifty students, including many of the town's most important citizens. The mayor's kids signed up along with many of the local merchants and their families. Apparently, a karate school filled a niche in Hammonton that had been empty for quite a while. We had a great group of dedicated students, and soon bonded into a family.

After we'd been open a few months, people started asking us to put on a demonstration. I thought it was a great idea and an excellent way to build registrations. I taught a few breaking techniques, we did some drills, practiced sparring and kobudo, and of course, kata. I had my students hand out flyers all over town. To my surprise, the demo was packed. There were even ten nuns from nearby St. Mary of Mount Carmel Catholic Church.

The chairs were set up around the perimeter, and the nuns were sitting front and center, in their customary habits with their coifs and wimples on their heads. One of the breaking demos we did was breaking a six-foot long two-by-two timber over my back. I would get in a *sanchin* stance, and one of the students would break the board across my back. One should always expect the unexpected, and although the wood behaved every time we practiced, this time a piece of the board went sailing straight for one of the nuns. She never lost her smile as the wood missed her head by inches and stuck the window behind her.

Thankfully, it had lost a lot of momentum by the time it hit the window and dropped harmlessly to the floor. I received a standing ovation, whether for the break or for my aim I never knew.

The real highlight of the night was Miko's Okinawan dance. She was dressed in her traditional Okinawan costume and danced flawlessly. She, too, received a standing ovation, and we got a big write-up in the local newspaper. Our karate school was the talk of the town, and our enrollment soared. Initially I was teaching children and adults together, but as classes grew I began to realize that was not a good idea. I separated the children's class from the adults' class; Miko teaching the kids and I teaching the adults. We trained the same way we trained in Okinawa, although at first I thought it might be a little intense for American students. However, the students loved it – they loved being pushed to achieve, and the school continued to thrive.

I RE-ENLIST

Things were going quite well; I was enjoying my job, my dojo and my community, but after about a year I started to get restless. I wanted to train some more with Sensei Nakazato, and I wanted to get my wife back with her family. But how could I leave my students? As I mentioned, we had all become one big family, and I knew they would not be happy to hear I was leaving. If I just closed the dojo, I would be betraying their trust in me; they would not have joined and stuck it out if they had not believed I would be with them for the long haul. I needed Bob Herten again! So I picked up the phone.

"Sensei Herten, I need to go back to Okinawa. I need to continue my training, and my wife would like to be back with her family. Do you have any black belts who would like to move to Hammonton and take over my dojo?"

"I can't promise anything, but I'll talk to my black belts. It may take a week or so, but I'll call you back as soon as I have something for you."

He was as good as his word. A week later he called me back and said he had two young black belts who were very good; they were not married, they were ready to run a school, and he thought it would work out for everybody. They moved down about a month before I left and helped with the instruction in my dojo. I wanted to make the transition as easy as I could for my Hammonton students. They were a great bunch, that first group of students, and I think of them to this day.

My first assignment after re-enlisting in the Air Force was Dover Air Force Base in Dover, Delaware. I was assigned to the base hospital as a medic. We lived in base housing, and after we settled in for a few weeks I began to look for a place to teach karate. I was offered the Youth Center. The base newspaper published an article about my wife and me, highlighting our martial arts background. When we opened, we had fifty kids sign up!

The kids were soon joined by adult GIs and their wives, and I again had to split the group into adults' classes and children's classes. But even then, I was getting more students than I could comfortably handle (remember, I still had my Air Force duties as well), so I called Frank Hargrove for advice. Sensei Hargrove had a dojo in Virginia with way more students than I had, and he was managing quite well. He said he's come to the base and observe, and then give me the benefit of his experience.

Frank came and watched a class. I thought I would receive major compliments, because I was sure I was doing everything right. Wrong.

I was teaching the way they taught in Okinawa. For example, when my students were doing kata, I was doing the same kata, full force, in front of the class. By the time we were finished my *gi* was wringing wet. A great example for my students, but a very ineffective way to teach, as I soon found out. After class I sat down with Frank and asked what he thought. I knew he would be impressed.

"Are you kidding?" Frank asked.

"No, my students see that I'm working as hard as they are. That's important."

"What's more important is that you know what your students are doing. Do you know what the white belt in the fourth row was doing? He was doing the whole kata backwards. When the class turned right, he turned left. And the girl in the yellow belt didn't do a single cat stance; she did front stances instead. You're teaching, not working out. You have to be watching your students constantly, so you know what needs correcting. If you want to work out, do it on your own time, not on your students' time."

Wow! I deeply appreciated Frank's "frank" assessment of my class and implemented his suggestions immediately. Classes ran much more smoothly and I had no problem with the volume of students. I soon became good friends with Sensei Hargrove; my wife and I would visit his dojo often, and he taught me a great deal – not just about karate and how to run a class, but about life in general.

MY FIRST TOURNAMENT

One of my wife's Okinawan girlfriends lived on McGuire Air Force Base, and we would often go visit on weekends. While Miko and her friend were out shopping and doing "girl stuff," I would go to the base gym and shoot hoops with my sons. In a room adjacent to the basketball court there was a kung-fu class, and many times I'd stop to watch. I had to admit, they were pretty impressive. I was especially impressed

Robert Teller presenting Jimmy Teller (6 years old) first place in forms and sparring at his first tournament.

with the instructor, a gentleman named S.L. Martin. One day when Master Martin was not there, I started talking to one of the senior students. He told me Master Martin was a master sergeant in the Air Force and began his martial arts training in Okinawan karate. In the mid-fifties he studied with Sensei Nagamine and with Master Soken. Master Martin's last two tours of duty were in Taiwan, and that's where he became involved with kung-fu. He told me they were having a tournament the next Saturday and I should come watch. I might also have an opportunity to speak with Master Martin.

The next week, I drove back to McGuire by myself to watch the tournament. One of Master Martin's senior students introduced me to him, and I mentioned that I earned my black belt in Okinawa. I also told him I'd seen some of his kung-fu classes and I was quite impressed.

I learned, however, that tournaments in America are completely different from Okinawan tournaments. In Okinawa it's all about the karate. The preliminary meeting is short because everyone knows the rules. There is no need to introduce each black belt individually. And the first-place trophies are about a foot tall. The tournament starts when it's scheduled to start, prizes are distributed, and the whole thing lasts a few hours, tops.

In the U.S., it seemed like it was all about the pageantry. The black belt meeting could last an hour or more, because every dojo operated under a different set of rules. The black belts would all line up and be introduced individually – it could take hours before the actual competition began! And after it was over, the trophies – sometimes as tall as four feet or more – would be handed out in an elaborate ceremony; every first- second- and third-place winner was called up by name. A tournament scheduled start was 9:00 am could last until eight or nine in the evening. Needless to say, I was astonished.

When Master Martin's tournament was over, I thanked him and told him it really opened my eyes. He suggested I hold a tournament of my own – that it was an excellent way to get my school known – and that if I needed any help to give him a call. By the time I got home I decided I was going to hold a tournament at the base. The trouble is, I had no idea how to go about it. I called Frank Hargrove and told him my thoughts.

"Robert, do you think you're ready or something that big yet? It takes a lot of planning and a lot of experience. Don't you think you should wait awhile?"

"Too late! I already got permission to use the base gym, and a date. My name's pretty well known around the base and I think I'll do alright."

"Well, you'd better make some flyers and start sending them out to every karate school in the area. Good luck!"

Not only did I send my flyers to area schools, I sent them to schools in other states. Dover Delaware is close to Pennsylvania, New Jersey and Maryland, and there's no reason competitors might not come from any of them. Then I started to get nervous, and I called Master Martin. He laughed and said that he had been a little nervous before his first tournament too.

He said he remembered I trained in Okinawa, and asked who I had studied with. He knew all my teachers. He suggested that we could have a joint workout with his students and mine, and I said, "Why don't you come to Dover next Saturday?"

We had a great workout, and I realized that there's more to martial arts than Okinawan karate. I was really impressed with his students and the quality of his kung-fu. I was nowhere near his level of skill and experience, and to this day I wonder why he took an interest in me. But I'm grateful that he did! After the workout we started to talk about my tournament.

"Where are you getting your trophies?"

"I have no idea. I thought I'd check to Yellow Pages for trophy shops."

"No need; I've already done that. I get my trophies from Spike's Trophies in Chinatown in Philadelphia. You'd better call them as soon as possible because it takes time to make the trophies. They're a busy shop."

Bottom line: Master Martin not only helped me organize the tournament, he set it up and ran it for me. Thank goodness – because I had no idea how involved this tournament business could be.

Then another challenge arose. I was supposed to pick up the trophies the Thursday before the Saturday of the tournament, but I only had a tiny car and couldn't possibly fit all those trophies in it. How was I going to get the trophies back to Dover? Then it hit me. We had two ambulance runs every week. On Tuesdays we would take patients to the hospital at Andrews Air Force base in Maryland. On Thursdays we would take patients to the Philadelphia Naval Hospital. These trips were for the patients that had to see specialists that we didn't have at the tiny Dover base hospital. I signed up for the Thursday run.

The ambulance held six passengers (plus a long area in the back for a litter), but I only had three. I dropped the patients off at the Naval Hospital at 9:00 and told them I'd be back to pick them up at 2:00. Then I drove the ambulance to Chinatown and parked it in front of the trophy store. I couldn't park a government ambulance in a parking lot, and I expected to get a ticket parking on the street, but what choice did I have? Then I started loading the trophies. There were so many boxes of trophies they wouldn't all fit back in the litter area; I had to put some on the patients' seats. I was thinking, "Now where are my patients going to sit?"

But I got my trophies and escaped without a ticket, so it was back to the Naval Hospital to pick up my guys. I arrived promptly at 2:00, and the patients helped me rearrange the boxes so everyone fit. We even made room for the third patient on the front seat. When we got back to base I drove straight to my house, where the patients helped me unload packages, laughing that no one would believe them if they told them about the trip. I laugh about it too, now… but at the time it was a nightmare.

The day before the tournament I got a phone call from the base gym: Did I want them to sell food at the tournament?

"Do you usually sell food at events like this?"

"Yeah, food sells pretty well."

"Then sell it."

"Do you want us to sell beer?"

"Do you usually sell beer?"

"Well, we sell beer at all the basketball games."

"Okay, sell beer too."

Big mistake, as you'll find out soon.

The day of the tournament arrived and the place was packed – it was standing room only. Some of the biggest names in karate on the East Coast were in attendance. For my very first tournament! I couldn't believe my eyes. The black belt meeting was run by Master Martin and Master Hargrove, and it's a good thing – many of the black belts were asking questions that I had no idea what they were talking about. My wife and some of her friends were handling registration and collecting the money, and it looked like they had been doing it all their lives. Master Martin was in charge, and even though it was supposed to be my tournament, I was little more than his gofer. But I was having a ball! And to top it off, my six-year-old son Jimmy took first place in his division. What could go wrong?

Remember the beer?

When the tournament was about halfway over, I noticed that some of the spectators were getting a little rowdy. As the tournament progressed they got louder and louder until, by the time the black belt fighting division got underway, they started coming out of the stands onto the floor whenever they disagreed with a call. Pretty soon it was an all-out brawl. Thank goodness for Master Hargrove and Master Martin! Drunk GIs were flying out of the ring as fast as they came rushing in. Soon base security arrived and escorted the drunk spectators off the premises. I learned a lot of things at that tournament, but none more important than this: NEVER, EVER SERVE BEER.

5
BACK TO THE SOURCE

At that time I was still in my twenties, and young men tend to have an inflated sense of self-importance. I was a black belt! I could do anything! But the fact is, I had only just learned to crawl. At the *kyu* levels, a karate student is learning the basic moves and developing muscle memory. First degree black belt signifies you've learned the rudiments and you're ready to begin to learn the art. After all, there are ten degrees of black belt, so first degree is the bottom step. Too many young men get their black belt and then leave their instructors to start their own school. But how can you teach something you've only just begun to learn yourself? I was beginning to realize that despite my shiny new black belt, I had much, much more to learn.

When I first arrived at Dover I requested re-assignment in Okinawa, but it had been over a year and I heard nothing. I started going to the personnel office every week to ask them when I would be re-assigned. I told them my wife's mother was very sick. I told them anything I could think of to expedite my orders back. They finally got tired of seeing my face every week and gave me a number to call at Air Force headquarters in Texas. I redoubled my efforts, and called not once, but twice every week. I always got a different person. Then one day I hit pay dirt. I happened to reach a sergeant who really seemed to want to help me. He also had a Japanese wife, and he had studied martial arts in Japan. I gave it everything I had… and two weeks later I had my orders. I was going back to Okinawa!

My orders were for Kadena, and we got off-base housing in Misato-shi, Awase, the very same town I lived in when I started training with Sensei Kise and Master Soken. There was a waiting list for on-base housing that went by rank. The advantages of being housed on base were that you were usually close to your work, the houses were very modern, and you didn't have to pay rent or utilities. We were told that we might qualify for on-base housing in six months to a year.

I couldn't wait to see Sensei Nakazato again. At the first opportunity, I drove to his house with my wife and kids, bringing some gifts I had brought him and his wife from the U.S. He was happy to see us again; I told him I couldn't wait to start training, and asked if Jimmy could train too. Jimmy was seven years old and had a good karate background. Sensei Nakazato said Jimmy was welcome to train but he would have to come when other Okinawan kids were there. We started our training the following week.

Even though it was an hour's drive each way, we trained five nights a week and sometimes on Saturday. Only on Wednesdays, kobudo days, did Jimmy stay home. If the other Okinawan kids were gone by the time we arrived, Jimmy would have to sit and wait for me. But while he was waiting, Sensei Nakazato managed to keep him busy. He had him do duck walks up and down to floor. He had him do sit-ups on a wooden slant board. Although he wasn't permitted to train on those nights, he was never idle.

REUNION WITH FRANK HARGROVE

One night, a few months after I returned to Okinawa in 1976, who should I see but Frank Hargrove, in the dojo with some of his students from the U.S.! I hadn't seen him in almost a year. Frank had been a student of Sensei Nakazato when he was in Okinawa as a member of the U.S. Air Force, from 1964 to 1967. During that time he became Sensei Nakazato's top American student. He was Nakazato's youngest fourth degree.

Frank Hargrove training in sword.

He returned to the United States in 1967, received his discharge from the Air Force, and then promptly returned to Okinawa to continue his karate training. While there, he enrolled in Jochi Daigaku University in Tokyo on the GI Bill, remaining for five years to earn his degree. During that time, he learned to speak fluent Japanese. Although it's quite a haul by boat from Tokyo to Okinawa, he returned at every opportunity to train with Sensei Nakazato. He returned to the U.S. shortly after he graduated from the university.

When I saw him in Sensei Nakazato's dojo, he told me he had brought his students for a karate tour of Okinawa. They were scheduled to return to the states the next day. Frank said he would love to stay a few weeks longer to train but he had nowhere to stay. I invited him to stay at my house. So for the next two or three weeks we went to Sensei Nakazato's dojo every night.

We used to spar together, but I couldn't get near him. Frank is much taller than me, and every time I launched an attack I was stopped by his much longer arms and legs.

"Frank, it's not a fair match. Look how much taller than me you are. How am I supposed to get in on you?"

"In a real fight on the street, you can't choose your opponent by height, can you?" he said. "It's not a matter of height, it's all in the technique. Timing. Speed. Angles. I used to spar with Okinawans far shorter than you who used to kick my butt. Don't give up – you'll get it!"

He started teaching me about angles, and about picking up subtle clues as to your opponent's intent. My karate improved a hundred percent.

One day we left my house for the dojo a little earlier than usual to try to beat the traffic. No such luck; the traffic was already at a standstill. As we sat there in the gridlock, we talked karate and reminisced about the old days. Suddenly, out of nowhere, a car smacked into the rear passenger side of my car. The two young Okinawans in the other car got out and helped push my car out of the way, and Frank ran to a local store to ask them to call the police. I told the pair from the other car that the police were on their way, and we all sat and waited.

When the police arrived they first went to the Okinawan guys and asked what happened. The police and the two guys were speaking Japanese and I didn't understand a word. But Frank did! They were telling the cops that the accident was all my fault. Frank jumped out of the car, ran over to the police, and said they were lying; that it was them, not us, who caused the accident. The two Okinawans' jaws dropped; they never imagined that an American could be that fluent in Japanese. By that time there were a lot of bystanders around who had witnessed the accident, and they all corroborated Frank's account – that the accident was the fault of the other driver. If Frank had not been there I would have been charged with the accident. Then, when the police officer asked Frank where we were going, Frank told him that we were on our way to Sensei Nakazato's dojo. The officer got a big smile on his face.

Frank Hardgrove seated left of Master Nakazato; Robert Teller second row third from the right.

"Really? Sensei Nakazato was my karate teacher when I was in high school." The two Okinawan guys just shook their heads in disbelief.

MY SPLIT FROM SENSEI NAKAZATO

The drive from my house in Awase to Sensei Nakazato's dojo was becoming more and more unbearable. The traffic was getting worse and my son had started school again. It seemed like we were getting home later and later each night. My wife was upset because Jimmy was getting home too late on school nights and it was affecting his grades, and she told me to stop taking him to karate. I told her that Jimmy really enjoyed karate and I would see if Sensei Nakazato would let us go to Shiroma's dojo

Jiro Shiroma one of Sensei Nakazato's senior students and his dojo was in Futenma near the Futenma Marine Corps Air Station, just a twenty-minute ride from my house. One night after Sensei Nakazato's class, I stopped at Sensei Shiroma's dojo on my way home. I explained my situation and asked him if I could train with him.

He smiled and said, "Sensei Nakazato will not let you train with me."

I asked if it was all right for me to ask Sensei Nakazato. He smiled again and said yes, if it was okay with Sensei Nakazato I'd be more than welcome. But I could tell by his expression on his face he knew what the outcome would be.

At the next afternoon class, I decided to ask Sensei Nakazato if I could train at Sensei Shiroma's dojo. The afternoon class was usually small, two or three students. With the help of one of the English-speaking Okinawan students, I told Sensei Nakazato about the long travel time and Jimmy's need to get home earlier. I told him with his permission I would continue to train on Saturdays at his dojo. I thought for sure he would understand. But to my surprise he got very angry and told me I train with him or nowhere! I remember getting a queasy feeling and I couldn't look at him in the face. It's the last time we ever talked.

When I got home that night, I told Miko what had happened. It was very hard for me because I really enjoyed Sensei Nakazato and his dojo. After a few days of soul searching, I decided to look for another dojo near my home. I wanted my son to be able to continue training with me.

Way back when, when I left Sensei Kise and started looking for a dojo, I accidently found Katsuyoshi Kanei Sensei's dojo. It was in the village of Chibana, near Kadena Air Force Base. Sensei Kanai taught a Gōjū-ryū style. I had gone a couple of times to watch the classes. One thing that impressed me most about Sensei Kanei is that I would see him sitting in his house working with his son on school work. When they finished they would enter the dojo together and the karate class would begin. It was a very small school but the classes were very structured and hard! Every student was sweating.

Now, in search of another karate school, I thought of Sensei Kanei. I thought I would give Sensei Kanie's Gōjū-ryū a try. But when I went to where his dojo used to be, he had moved. The people who lived there gave me the address of his new home and dojo, which turned out to be quite large and modern compared to his earlier headquarters. I couldn't meet with him that day, but managed to talk with him a few days later. My wife told him about my situation with Sensei Nakazato, and that I wanted to continue training with my son. He smiled and told me I could start training the following week. His small little dojo had grown into a big school with many Okinawan students but very few Americans.

I was a white belt again, but it didn't bother me as long as I was learning the real thing. I was not there for rank, but to learn karate. The training was completely different than what I was used to. There was a lot of body conditioning and many more repetitious karate drills. It was like learning to walk all over again. I remember leaving there each night feeling like a beginner in the martial arts. The footwork and punching was completely different than what I was accustomed to. Would I ever be able to learn this new style of karate? My son didn't help matters, because he was picking everything up so fast that on occasion I would be asking him questions.

On certain nights Sensei Kanei would not be in class, and his class would be taught by a senior student. I don't remember the student's name, but I recall that he was very soft spoken and a very good teacher. He was short in stature but a hardnosed, no-nonsense instructor. He used to walk around the classroom with a twelve-inch wooden stick, hitting arms and legs while he taught. Sometimes he would hit the students in certain parts of their bodies to make sure they were tight and in the proper stance. I later found out later that Sensei Kanei studied *kobudo* with Sensei Shinpo Matayoshi, and the nights he was not in class he was in Naha city studying it.

My Gōjū-ryū classes seemed like they were never going to end. The transition from Shōrin-ryū to Gōjū-ryū was difficult, and some of the principles seemed directly opposite. I just didn't like the hard style of Gōjū-ryū. I guess I had been doing the more fluid style of Shōrin-ryū too long. I only lasted six months at Sensei Kanei's dojo. Looking back, I wish I had stuck it out a little longer because I realize it takes a long time to transition from one system to another. There are a lot of habits to unlearn. If taught and learned correctly, Gōjū-ryū is a strong and effective martial art.

Robert Teller in Vietnam 1968

Robert Teller and cousin Jim Bunting in Chu Lai, Vietnam

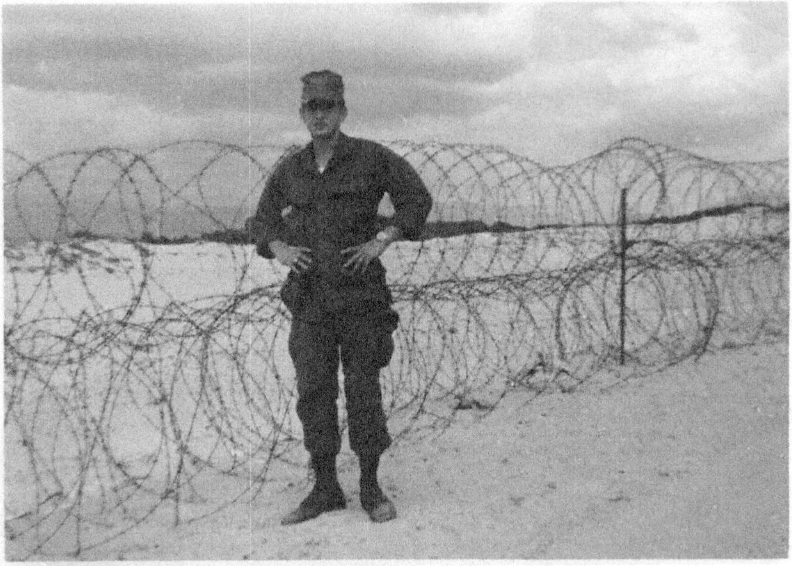

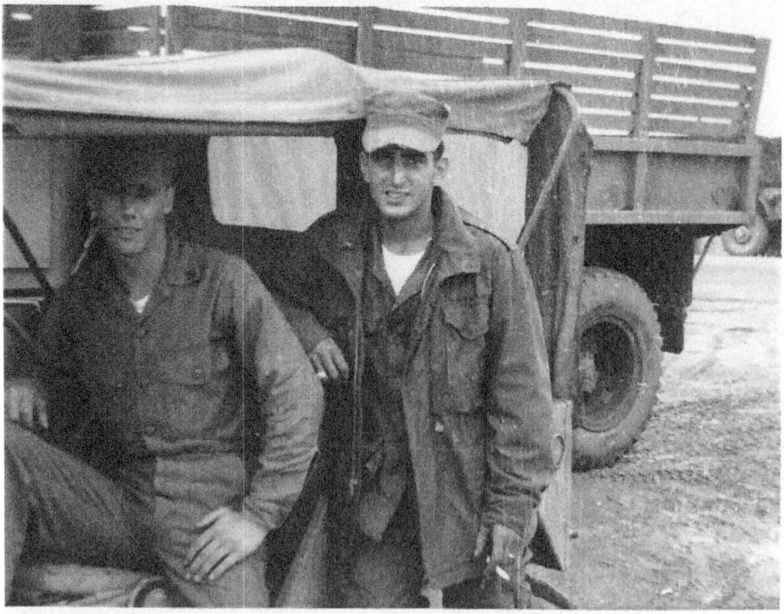

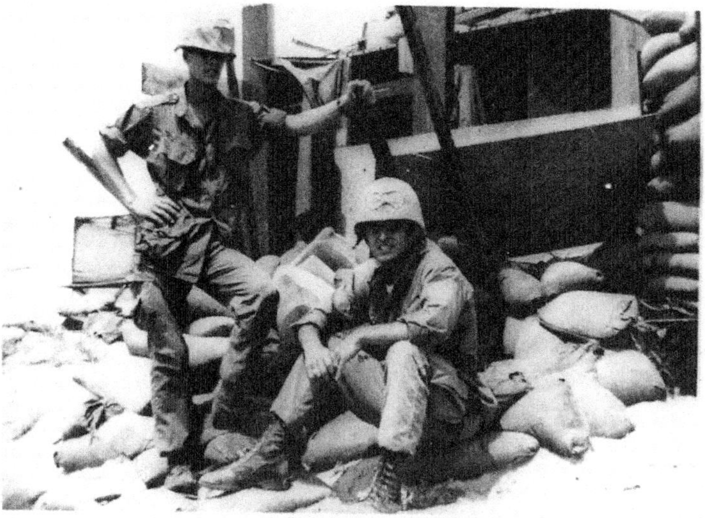

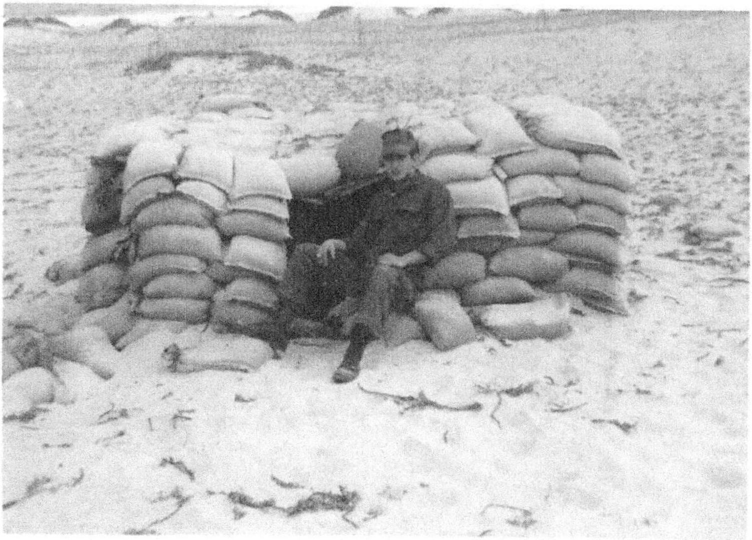

Grandmaster Hohan Soken's patch

Grandmaster Hohan Soken

Master Fusei Kise with Robert Teller and one of Master Kise's students

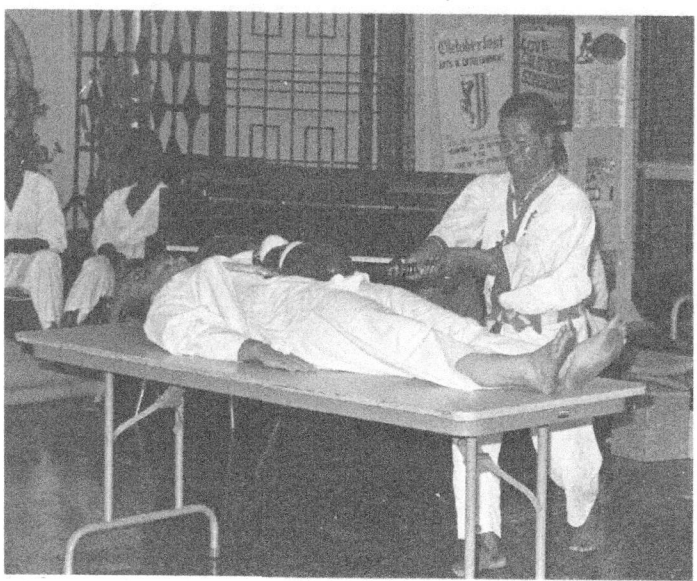

Master Kise cutting a melon on a student's stomach

Karate class flyer hung up on Naha Airbase

Master Fusei Kise's first karate dojo

Master Nakazato correcting Frank Hardgrove's form

One of Master Nakazato's students hitting a makiwara board

Master Shugoro Nakazato's afternoon class

Master Shugoro Nakazato with nunchaku

Robert Teller interviewing Master Shosei Kina with Father Ikehara translating for the Okinawan Passtime Magazine.

Picture taken in Master Shosei Kina's living room.

Master Shinyu Isa demonstrating kobudo weaponry in his dojo.

Master Masanobu Kina with kobudo master, Matsutaro Ire

Master Matsutaro Ire was a known kobudo practitioner, famous for his expertise in the kama. Master Shian Toma studied under Master Matsutaro Ire to learn the kama.

Master Masanobu Kina

公会流空手道場練芸館昇段級授与式　1969年1月1日

Master Masanobu Kina's karate class of 1969

Master Masanobu Kina and Robert Teller kobudo training

Master Kyan Shinei and Master Masanobu Kina visiting high school karate club

Robert Teller participates in the Bunkasai Culture Festival, becoming part of the first group of Americans to do so.

Master Masanobu Kina performing Shimabuku Passai at the Bunkasai Festival

Master Masanobu Kina's granddaughter, far left, following in her grandfather's footsteps. 1st place in female team kata.

Tomo Kuda training with student as his father, Yuichi Kuda, looks on.

Author Robert Teller sparring with soon to be brother-in-law Ron Nix, and performing kata for his Yondan test.

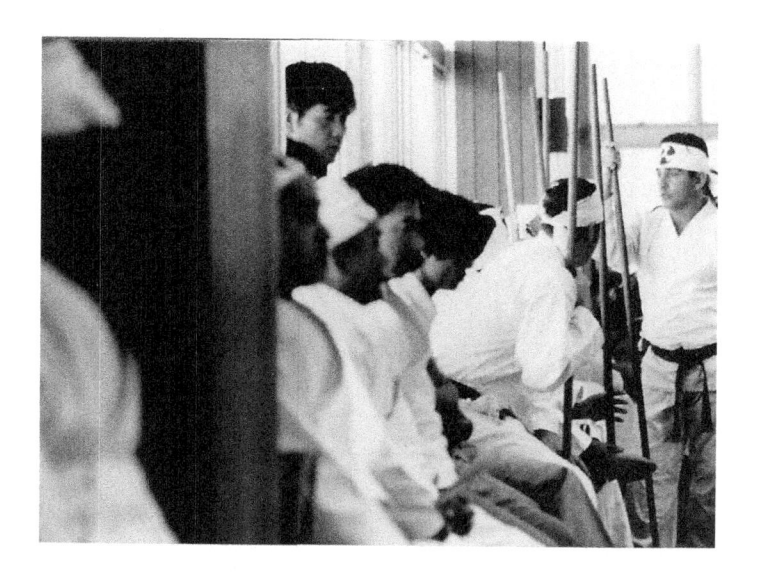

Master Masanobu Kina sitting with Master Seiki Arakaki and his wife.

Robert Teller with Grandmaster Seikichi Uehara and Master Shian Toma of Motobu-Ryu.(later Seidokan)

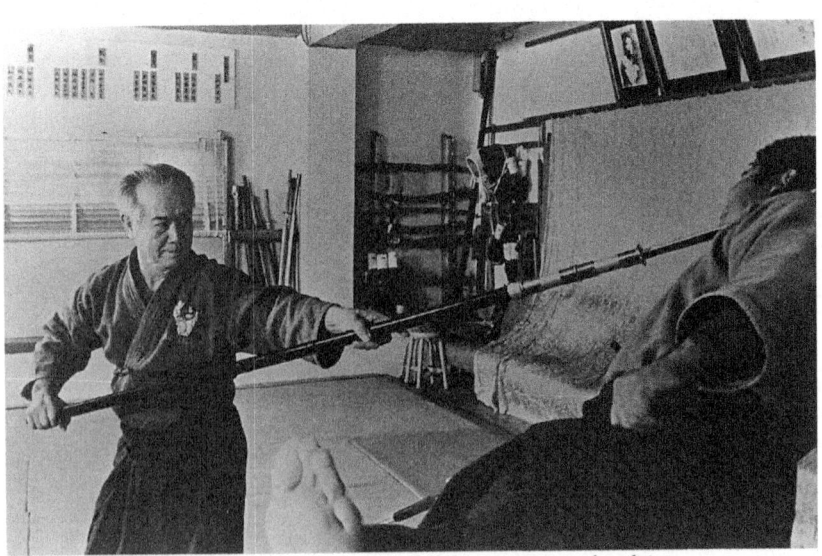

Seikichi Uehara training with the naginata in his dojo

Special training with Master Shian Toma with Seidokan black belts.

Robert Teller with Masters, Shian Toma and Master S.L. Martin.

Master Shian Toma training on the beach

Master Shian Toma giving instruction in sword techniques

Robert Teller demonstrating the use of the chishi (an Okinawan weight training device) that was given to him by Grandmaster Hohan Soken from his dojo.

This bokken was given to Robert Teller August 1987 by Grandmaster Seikichi Odo.

Taika Seiyu Oyata performing a technique on Robert Teller's senior student, Lee Stowe.

Taika Oyata meeting with Philadelphia Eagles's all pro linebacker, William Thomas.

Taika Seiyu Oyata, early morning training with Masaya Kudaka

Traditional Japanese wedding picture, author Robert Teller and Kiyoko Miko Teller

Kiyoko Teller performs naginata dance.

Kiyoko Teller teaching class at Dover Air Force Base.

Master Shinpo Matayoshi teaching my wife the naginata.

My son Jimmy Teller and I at Katsuren Castle.

The author on the steps of Nakagusuku Castle.

The author and his wife with their two sons Scotty and Jimmy Teller.

Author's daughter, Naomi Tina (Teller) Cho demonstrating use of the Okinawan weapon the techu. Normally used by females, the weapon would be concealed in the sleeves of the kimono.

Left to Right: Niko Teller, Jimmy Teller, Robert Teller, and Julian Teller

Robert Teller with sons and grandsons

Author Robert Teller being awarded hachi-dan (Eighth degree black belt)

From Left to Right: Ron Nix, Akemi Nix, Robert Teller, Jimmy Teller, John Anthony, and Levi Wolf

6

THE PICTURE OF SHOSEI KINA

My two boys played little league football on base. Each team was named after a professional NFL team; there were the Dallas Cowboys, the Cleveland Browns, etc. Our team was the Pittsburgh Steelers. Their games were played on Saturday mornings. There was kind of an informal competition among the fathers: we would paint our kids' helmets so each week they'd look shiny and new. Each father would try to outdo the other fathers in making their kid's helmet look the best.

One Friday after work I was looking for something that I needed for the helmet. I don't remember exactly what it was, but they didn't have what I was looking for at the Base Exchange so I decided to go off base and look for it at the local hardware store. I parked my car and started walking up the street toward the hardware store when I noticed a big picture of an old karate master in the window of a small photography store. He was in his karate uniform and he was wearing a gold belt. I thought I knew all of the old masters on Okinawa – I was a karate history buff! But I didn't recognize this master. Who was he? I decided to go into the photo store and find out.

Master Shosei Kina

Unfortunately, the owner of the store did not speak any English. With my limited Japanese, I got it across to the owner that I wanted to know who the karate master was in the picture. He ran to the back of the store and got his wife to come out front to watch the store. Then he gestured to me to follow him, as he began half walking, half running down the street and down small alleys. I could barely keep up with him. We finally came to a small karate school. All the writing on the door was in Japanese. Nobody was at the school so the man knocked on the door of the attached house. A woman came out, and she didn't speak English either. They both pointed to the class times on the door and indicated I should come back when the school was open.

That night I returned to the school with my wife. There were about a dozen kids there, but no sensei. One of the kids told my wife he wasn't there yet; sometimes he comes late. We waited as long as we could, but we had to pick up my kids at my wife's parents' house. On our second visit to the karate school, the sensei was there. His name was Shinju Isa, and he looked to be a few years older than me. He was short but solidly built; he had that look that many Okinawan karate senseis do – you didn't want to get him mad!

We didn't know it at the time, but he was in the middle of becoming a Buddhist Monk. He eventually went on to graduate from the *Shingen-So Somoto-San Denpo* monastery in Kyoto, Japan and went on to be one of the head directors at the Futenma Temple. That was why he was often late and sometimes didn't show up at all. My wife told Sensei Isa I was a karate history buff and I had seen a picture of an old sensei that I didn't recognize. He said the picture was his sensei, Shosei Kina, in his nineties and still very alert. We stayed for over an hour, and he gave me a lesson on Okinawan karate and Okinawan history like I never heard before. He was very intelligent man and a fascinating story teller, even though he didn't speak much English. I could have listened to him all day.

I asked him what style of karate he taught and he replied, Shōrin-ryū. I thought, "This is great! I finally found a style of karate that I'm comfortable with and a teacher who's into the history." It was also a mere five minutes from my house. I asked him in English if my son and I could train with him. He laughed and said he didn't speak much English; my wife told him what I had said and he replied certainly, I could start tomorrow.

Sensei Isa was heavily into kobudo, and he had weapons that I had never seen before. He showed me an old pair of nunchaku made from the bridle of a horse. They eventually

Master Shinyu Isa holding the techu.

evolved into two smaller straight pieces of wood joined together by a cord, which were much easier to manipulate. He showed me what the original tonfa looked like; it was a handle to turn a small gristmill. Gripped by the handle, with the longer length tucked under the arm, the weapon is for the most part concealed, but the knobbed end can inflict painful injuries when jabbed into an adversary, and of course the weapon could be quickly spun around to use the longer end as a baton. He also showed me a weapon called *techu*. The techu was a small, fist-size weapon carried by women and concealed under their sleeves of a kimono, almost like a wooden brass knuckle. If attacked, a woman trained in the use of the techu could use the weapon to gouge the eyes and cause painful injury to the face and groin. Even most of the other Okinawan karate masters I had asked never heard of the techu. Okinawan weapons almost all evolved from farm implements, because the Japanese overlords did not allow Okinawans to own weapons.

We didn't waste any time; we started to train with Sensei Isa the next day. Jimmy and I were the only two Americans in the dojo. The kids' class was first, and when it was time for bogu kumite they all wanted to spar with Jimmy. They took turns, one after another, and when the bogu kumite was over Jimmy was so exhausted he could barely stand up. It was a great bonding experience, and all the kids soon became Jimmy's friends.

Many nights sensei would not come 'til late. One night during the kids' class, Sensei was absent and the kids were being kids; there was a lot of horseplay going on. Suddenly Sensei walked in and the kids immediately came to attention. You could've heard a pin drop. Sensei expected the classes to run normally even when he was not there, and he was not happy! He had all the kids line up in a *seiza* position, backs straight, eyes straight, without moving a muscle!

Sensei had a little tatami mat area off to the side of the dojo, where he would often hold mini meetings with his black belts. He had one of his meetings that night, while the kids were sitting in seiza. We must have been sitting there for an hour, and those kids did not move. Then he got up and walked slowly over to the kids. He began to talk to them for what seemed to be a half hour. Then he had them bow and he slowly walked out of the dojo to get his gi on. When he was out of sight, the kids tried to get up but they couldn't walk. They were falling all over the room groaning in agony. I never saw the kid's horseplay again after that night.

One-night sensei told us that every year they celebrate *zen-nabe*. Long ago on Okinawa, whenever they didn't have rain for a long time and food became scarce, many people, especially young children, would starve. The people started eating anything they could find. The village would all work together and try to find anything that was edible: snakes, rats, lizards, etc., put it all in a big pot (*nabe*) and cook it all day. When it was time to eat, everybody had a small bowl; they would each get one scoop from the pot to eat. Today, although food is more plentiful, traditional Okinawans commemorate those days with a *zen-nabe* dinner.

On the night of our *zen-nabe* dinner, all the kids in the dojo had a bowl, and they all got in line reluctantly to wait their turn. Whatever sensei scooped into their bowl they had to eat. I'm sure Sensei put nothing but wholesome food in the *nabe*, but it was amusing watching the kids choke down their mystery meal. The practice has a moral: be thankful for what you have.

One evening, sensei called a meeting of his black belts, and when I walked into the dojo he invited me over to the table. There were four or five black belts there who were unfamiliar to me. I sat down at the small table in a seiza position and Sensei began talking in Japanese. Sensei loved to talk! Again, he was talking for almost an hour and I didn't understand a word he said. Since I wasn't used to sitting in seiza for so long, my legs began to fall asleep. I tried to reposition them, but to no avail; I was numb from the waist down. Then I decided to stretch my legs out straight.

As soon as I did, one of the black belts jumped over the table and was ready to start pounding on me. Thankfully, Sensei Isa jumped in to intervene.

He said in Japanese, "It's okay, he's an American and he is not fully familiar with our customs."

The Okinawan black belt said "He is being disrespectful!"

Sensei said, "He is still learning."

The black belts at that meeting all looked like they were *yakuza* (mafia)… very mean looking. I had never seen any of them train in the dojo. Luckily, that event ended the meeting, with no one (like me, for example) getting hurt. All the black belts left and sensei started to show me some kobudo.

The adult class usually consisted of only a few students. Among them was a young Chinese student in his early twenties. He wore a brown belt and was there almost every class. Many nights it was just the two of us, and we would mostly work on kata. He spoke pretty good English, as well as Chinese and Japanese; he had gone to the Okinawan Christian High School which was taught in English. He said his parents were from Taiwan and owned a Chinese restaurant, and sometimes he had to work at the restaurant and couldn't make it early.

He usually came for the kid's class, so if sensei wasn't there he would teach. Whether sensei was there or not, the class would start with the kids running barefoot through the streets chanting something in Japanese. It was about a mile run and Jimmy and I would always run with them. Jimmy hated to run, and I hated to run barefoot; I was always running into dog shit and pebbles. I had very sensitive feet.

When it was just the Chinese student and myself (my wife would pick Jimmy up after class), I would often ask him questions about sensei Isa and the style of karate that he taught. One night when we were alone I asked him if he ever met Sensei Kina.

"Which one?" he asked.

"Are there two Sensei Kinas? The one who's Sensei Isa's teacher."

He said he had never met Shosei Kina, Isa's teacher, but he had a friend who had studied with Masanobu Kina. He said that Masanobu Kina and Shosei Kina were distant cousins. They were from the same village and lived a few doors away from each other. Masanobu Kina was much younger then Shosei Kina but about ten or fifteen years older than Sensei Isa. When he was much younger, he had attended a couple of Masanobu Kina's classes with his friend at a church in Shimabuku village. It was pretty close to where we were. He said he didn't think Masanobu Kina was still teaching there but a friend of his father's would know. His name was Father Sadao Ikehara and he was an Episcopal priest, the head of the first nursing home on Okinawa, run jointly by all the Christian churches on Okinawa. He said that Father Ikehara was one of Masanobu Kina's black belts. I wrote down his name and thought "What a great piece of information this is. There are more karate masters than I ever heard of!" The nursing home was very close to my house, so on my way home that night, I drove by it.

THE FIRST NURSING HOME ON OKINAWA

The custom in Okinawa was that when the parents got old and retired, the oldest son and wife take over the house and care for the parents. Sometimes a small apartment-like addition is added on the main house for the parents to live in. After World War II, they started to find old people, sometimes in their nineties, both dead in their homes. What happened was a lot of the sons were killed during the war and many of the children relocated to mainland Japan. Some of the young daughters married American servicemen and moved to the United States. This left a lot of older parents without anybody to help take care of them. They were proud and didn't want anyone to know that they couldn't take care of themselves, so rather than ask for help they died in their homes. The Christian churches and missionaries in Okinawa decided to open a nursing home on to take care of the elderly who had no one else. This first nursing home was run by Father Ikehara, an Episcopalian priest who had gone to school for his theological education for ministry in the United States.

MY MEETING WITH SHOSEI KINA

After a week or so of not seeing Sensei Isa at the dojo, I decided to visit Father Ikehara at the nursing home. I wanted to learn more about Sensei Shosei Kina and get more information about Masanobu Kina. My wife and I went to the nursing home one day after I got off work, and my wife asked to see Father Ikehara. He wasn't there that day, but he would be in all the next day.

The next day we returned and met Father Ikehara. He was very soft spoken and easy to talk to. When my wife told him of my background in the martial arts, it became apparent that martial arts was one of his favorite subjects. He told us he knew Sensei Shosei Kina very well and would take me to visit him. He'd make the arrangements and get back to us. The next day he called and told my wife I could meet Sensei Kina on Friday after work, so I made a list of questions I wanted to ask. On Friday I went to the nursing home by myself; my wife had to work, but I really didn't need her because Father Ikehara spoke excellent English.

On the ride to Sensei Kina's house, I asked Father Ikehara how old Sensei Kina was. He replied, "Ninety-seven." I started to get a little nervous. He was ninety-seven years old? I didn't know what to expect. Father Ikehara said that Sensei Kina was very alert for his age. We parked the car and as we walked up to his house I was amazed at the beauty of the Japanese garden around his home. Father Ikehara said that Sensei Kina still worked on his garden every day.

When we arrived at the house, Sensei Kina's wife was at the door. She politely told us to come in and have a seat. We sat around a table in a small room and waited for Sensei Kina. When he arrived, I was in awe as he sat next to me.

"How do you explain your health, vitality, and longevity?" I asked.

"Vegetarianism, exercise, no smoking and no alcohol" He replied.

As our conversation continued he unveiled his past life as a student and teacher. At age eighteen he had become a teacher with a temporary certificate. His urge to be a teacher had been inspired in part by some good teachers he had as a boy. In 1904, when he was about twenty-one, Sensei Kina was warned that his certification for teaching was not adequate, that he must go to the normal school, and probably for the full four-year term. When he presented himself for what we might call placement testing, the results clearly showed that he was much more than prepared for the beginning of the four-year program. It was at this time his formal karate training began.

Master Shosei Kina with his wife in his garden.

He enrolled in the Okinawan Teacher College in Shuri, where he was introduced to his new karate instructor, the famous karate-ka Yasutsune Itosu. Sensei Itosu, who was about seventy-five years old at that time, held classes at the college once a week. Sensei Kina also added that at that time, karate students were expected to practice every day on their own. When Sensei Itosu would come in on the day of their lesson, he could tell by looking at their kata who had been studying the hardest.

Shortly after Sensei Kina began his karate training, Sensei Itosu retired from teaching at the college. Sensei Kina's karate instructor then became Itosu's top student, Kentsu Yabu. Kina related that after karate training they would often go visit Sensei Itosu and listen to him talk about karate. Sensei Kina's formal karate training lasted approximately five years under Sensei Yabu. Kina also studied the weapon called Sai from a famous Okinawan kobudo instructor, Kinjo Sanda, whose nickname was *Ufuchiku*, or Chief of Police, which was the top level of the *Shikusaji Pechin* class in Okinawan society. The title was reserved for senior police inspectors and chiefs. Ufuchiku was famous for his mastery of the sai and only taught a select few.

Before World War II brought Okinawa into the modern world, if you wanted to learn kobudo, you had to have a good karate foundation and permission from your karate instructor. Then you would go to a teacher that specialized in the weapon that you wanted to learn. There were no kobudo instructors who taught multiple weapons. If you wanted to learn the bo, you would go to a bo master. If you wanted to learn the kama, you would go to a sensei who taught the kama. The study of each specific weapon was an art in itself. You studied all of the elements of the weapon, not just kata. It took a lifetime to learn. Ufuchiku was a sai master   He did not teach any other weapons to Sensei Kina.

Sensei Kina went to Ufuchiku and asked if he could study with him. That was how things were done – you did not simply register and pay your money, you had to be accepted by the master. It was no sure thing.

Ufuchiku asked Sensei Kina, "How many men have you fought and beaten?"

It was an unexpected question. It was even more of a dilemma if the question meant he should give some kind of affirmative and informative answer. But he was not one to give the expected answer just so he would gain the privilege of training. So he simply said, "None."

Ufuchiku seemed to scoff and turned away.

Sensei Yabu, who was well acquainted with Ufuchiku and his ways, learned of the incident and interceded. Later Sensei Kina was given another hearing. This time there was no scoffing. Ufuchiku was even courteous. He told Kina that at the previous meeting he had simply been testing the young man. He wanted to be sure the aspiring student understood that the art was solely for defense and not for attack. So Sensei Kina was permitted to study the sai and eventually became Ufuchiku's top student.

As a school teacher, Kina was appointed to the Kishaba Elementary School in 1901, where he remained until 1916. Then from 1917 to 1923 he was with the Goeku School. In 1924, he returned to the Kishaba School as a junior high school teacher and remained there until the early 1930s. At age sixty he retired. During his teaching years, in addition to his classroom teaching, he instructed basic karate to the school karate club. He was often referred to as "the Karate Sensei" by the school pupils.

Sensei Kina's story was enlightening, but I knew there was even more in his past then he had revealed to me. Several magazine articles, (*Readers Digest*, etc.) had been written about him. Some of the following the material was gleaned from the enlightening book, "Why...To Okinawa?" written by W. Gordon Ross in 1971.

Ross relates the story of a meeting between a teen-aged Kina and a Christian missionary. Although the missionary's stay in Shimabuku village was brief, he had a profound influence on Kina's understanding of Christianity. This was Kina's only contact with a Christian. Sensei Kina and his closest friend Mojun Kina (no relation) read through the Japanese-language Bible the missionary left intently, and discovered an individual worth emulating and sound precepts on which to base a society. They taught Christianity with a fervor, and eventually converted the entire Shimabuku village.

Thirty years later, in 1945, the American army attacked the Japanese positions on Okinawa, and Shimabuku village took some heavy shelling. Aware of the American forces surrounding their area, the villagers met and decided they must move out and head north, away from the heavy fighting.

But Sensei Kina pointed out that that would create other problems. How would the feed themselves? Crops do not grow up overnight.

Ross quotes Kina as saying:

"Americans are gentleman. They will not harm civilians. War is between the military."

Then, startlingly, he offered to go out alone and face the troops. *"If the Americans threaten, I will step forward and die for you."*

And then it actually happened. An advance American patrol stormed the village of Shimabuku, guns leveled, ready to attack. That's when the two little old men approached, alone and unarmed, to meet the attackers. It was sixty-three-year-old Sensei Kina and his lifelong friend, fifty-seven-year-old Mojun Kina. Kina's now-famous words were,

Mojun Kina (Top) with Master Shosei Kina (Middle) with Thomas Higa (Bottom)

"You are American gentlemen. I am an Okinawan Christian."

The Americans were suspicious of a trick. They called for an interpreter, and Sergeant Thomas Higa came forward. Higa lived in Hawaii, but spent his early years in Okinawa. It was a truly amazing coincidence! Kina had been Higa's teacher in grade school, and they recognized each other at once! As they rushed weeping to embrace one another, the troops looked on in astonishment.

It was clear that this was no trick on the part of the Okinawans, and the troops lowered their arms and relaxed. It could have turned out differently, for Shimabuku village had indeed been marked for demolition. The Americans told the villagers that yes, they would have to vacate their village, but the American forces would provide both transportation and food. Kina was instructed to organize the villagers, appointing such personnel as police, administrators, etc.

The villagers were transported north, where they lived in caves and planted crops in nearby fields. At Kina's insistence, a school was built and provisions were made for the elderly around Ginoza, the area to which the villagers of Shimabuku were relocated. Thirty-eight years later, Emperor Hirohito presented Kina with the "*Kun Roku To*," or the "Sixth Order on Merit," for having saved the village. No other Okinawan had ever received this honor.

Master Shosei Kina, age 97, wearing the Kun Roku To.

In the early days of karate, before arrival of the Americans, there was no grading system in karate, so Kina was never afforded a rank. That was rectified in 1958, when Sensei Seikichi Uehara, grandmaster of Motobu-ryū karate, awarded him the rank of tenth degree black belt – karate's highest level – under the auspices of the All Okinawan Karate and Kobudo Rengokai.

Mr. Ross related that his final question to Sensei Kina was, "What does karate mean to you?"

In reply, Kina told the story of a past student, driven to be the best, who neglected his heath in his efforts to become the top academic student in his school. He lost weight and became sick and weak. Sensei Kina told him the he could not succeed without good health; to spend less time studying and devote more time to healthy eating, proper health practices, and exercise. That student, Shinei Kyan, took Sensei Kina's advice to heart and later became one of his top students. He also studied with Master Shoshin Nagamine and introduced kobudo into Nagamine's Matsubayashi-ryū system. Eventually he became Okinawa's representative to the National Diet of Japan (Japan's Congress).

Sensei Kina made it clear that he views karate as a way of life, enriching the mind and spirit as well as the body.

Looking over my notes from almost forty years ago it occurred to me that there were little things said by Sensei Kina that I didn't fully appreciate at the time. I was so intent on the meat of the story that I missed the profound wisdom about life's lessons that he was passing on to me. I now pass them on to my students.

1. *Hozo-tan-ren* (To perfect oneself): Sensei Kina said that this is very important in one's learning. When learning a new kata, only learn one part at a time. Don't try to repeat the whole lesson all at once. One section at a time until it is perfected.

2. *SAI*: When punching with the sai, don't rotate the hand. With a punch from the fist you rotate the hand for power. The sai has an iron tip; you don't have to rotate the weapon; you strike with the sai with a straight jab like punch.

3. THE PEN: As we neared the end the interview, I asked Father Ikehara if I could get Sensei Kina to autograph my book. He asked Sensei Kina and he said certainly. I handed Sensei Kina the book and a pen. When he started to sign the book, he took his time and seemed to be meticulous about his signature. When he finally finished, he handed me the book and I thanked him, but when I opened the book I couldn't find his signature. Father Ikehara and I searched the book, but no signature. Then my eye caught the pen I had given him and I noticed the top button had not been pushed. Ninety-seven-year-old men cannot see well; he couldn't see that he had written nothing! Father Ikehara told Sensei Kina and we all started laughing. Father Ikehara had a black Sharpie and Sensei Kina signed my book again. This time Father Ikehara asked for his *hanko* (personal signature stamp) and stamped my book.

4. THE CHAIR: After interviewing Master Kina, I asked Father Ikehara if I could take Sensei Kina's picture in his garden. Sensei Kina said yes but he would like his wife to be in the picture. I carried a chair out to the garden where Sensei Kina could sit. After all, he was ninety-seven years old! As I pointed for him to have a seat, he said politely, "I am a karate man, my wife can sit on the chair." Sensei Kina then tried to hold his wife's hand but she kept pulling it away (they don't like to show affection in public). Sensei Kina said to his wife in Japanese, "It's OK, he's an American." She smiled and he held her hand. Mrs. Kina was ninety-three years old.

5. HANDLE YOUR WEAPON EVERY DAY: At the time this lesson went right over my head! What he meant was, on the days he felt too lazy or ill to train, he always picked up his weapon anyway. When you touch it, you pick it up, and before you know it you're working out. He didn't mean this for karate only, but for life in general. As I write this book there are days even weeks that I can't get motivated to write. I now force myself to write at least one sentence every day (I "handle my weapon"). So far I have never been able to write only one sentence. The one sentence turns into paragraphs and the paragraphs into pages.

6. HOW MANY KARATE KATA DID YOU LEARN UNDER ITOSU SENSEI AND YABU SENSEI? I was told that in the old days a karate master would only teach one or two kata in a lifetime. I was very interested in how many kata Sensei Kina had learned. When I asked him how many kata he had learned, his reply to me was "over one hundred." I looked at Father Ikehara and said, "Over one hundred?" Father Ikehara again asked him, "How many kata?" He apologized and said he thought we meant *wazas* (combinations). He said that they had spent a lot of time learning different drills and techniques from the kata. Much emphasis was on kata training. I never did get an answer on how many and what

katas he learned. He started talking about the way they trained, and now I regret never getting him to answer my original question.

7
MASANOBU KINA

On the way home from Shosei Kina's house, I asked Father Ikehara if there was any chance of meeting Sensei Masanobu Kina as I was interested in training with him. Father Ikehara said Masanobu Kina was semi-retired from karate but we could go and see him at his house. He said he would get back to me and let me know when.

The following Saturday morning Father Ikehara and I went to Masanobu Kina's house. I was very nervous! As we walked through the gate to enter his house, there was a beautiful Japanese garden. I later found out it was one of sensei Kina's many hobbies. There was barely enough room to walk up to his house with all the bonsai trees and beautiful flowers that lined the walkway. The sliding doors to the house were open and Sensei Kina was sitting at a little table drinking tea. Father Ikehara introduced me to Sensei Kina and he never cracked a smile, which made me even more uneasy.

Father Ikehara began talking to Sensei Kina, and as they talked I look around the room in amazement. There must have been a hundred seashells all around the rooms on shelves. They were mainly conch shells of different sizes. He had cleaned and polished all the shells to a beautiful finish – another hobby. I was told later that he would usually go to the beach on Saturday mornings looking for shells. After becoming his student, I would often accompany him to the beach on Saturdays and we would train in the water.

Father Ikehara began asking me the questions that Sensei Kina had asked him. How long had I been training in the martial arts, who had I studied with, etc.? After filling him in about my background in karate, I told him that my last teacher was Sensei Isa. I told him I quit going there because he was in the process of becoming a Buddhist monk, and he was hardly ever at the dojo. Sensei Kina quickly replied that Sensei Isa had been his student. I thought it best that I didn't say anything more about Sensei Isa.

Sensei Kina's wife then brought us some tea and snacks. After about an hour of talking, Father Ikehara said we could meet with Sensei Kina a couple of times a week at his house and train. I said I would be honored, and how soon can we start? They both laughed and said Monday, six o'clock.

Masanobu Kina at age 8 (boy with the white hat) with his father Shomo (standing) and Grandfather Shojin Kina

On Monday I arrived a little early. Father Ikehara hadn't arrived yet, but as soon as Sensei Kina saw me we started to work out. The area he took me to was in the middle of his Japanese garden, about eight feet by eight feet, barely enough room for one person to do a kata. It was a little awkward because Sensei Kina only knew a few words of English and my Japanese was no better. We were both speaking the language of karate!

One thing I liked about training with Sensei Kina: there was not a lot of talking. We did a lot of punches, kicks and blocks, followed by a form of yakusoku kumite. Father Ikehara arrived about thirty minutes later and joined us. Now, with the help of Father Ikehara, Sensei Kina could tell me the difference between the way I did certain techniques and the way he did them. He drilled us for over an hour non-stop. My gi was soaking wet when we were done.

We continued to work out in his garden for a little over a month. One day when Father Ikehara arrived, he started talking to Sensei Kina in Japanese.

Then he turned to me and said, "How would you like to start a dojo in the nursing home where I work? My younger brother works there as a cook." He said his brother and a few other Okinawans actually live at the nursing home and would love to do karate with us. Sensei Kina said I should bring my children, he would bring his children, and we could have a little dojo in the recreation room.

I replied "Great! How soon can we start?"

Déjà vu! They both laughed and said "Monday, six o'clock!"

The recreation room at the nursing home was huge; it was used for birthday parties, holiday celebrations, meetings and workshops during the day. We had about ten students at our first workout. I said I would collect money from the students to pay Sensei Kina, and how much money I should I collect? If I remember correctly it was about fifteen or twenty dollars a month per student.

One thing I often think about, after all these years: when I collected the money from the students and tried to give it to Sensei Kina, he would always tell me to put it in the donation box of the nursing home. When I go to Okinawa I always visit Sensei Kina's family. On one trip I was telling one of his daughters how he always told me to put the money in the donation box. She told me her father never took money for teaching karate because he felt that he was still a learner, not ready yet to become a fulltime teacher. He was probably one of the greatest teachers I ever had!

Sensei Kina worked us hard and within a month, we had about twenty or twenty-five students. Some were friends of mine from the Air Force base, some were Okinawan kids from the nearby neighborhood, and even Sensei Kina's daughters started to train with us. It was a nice atmosphere because it was about half Okinawans and half Americans. The Japanese kids were learning English and the Americans were learning Japanese.

In the first few months, Sensei Kina drilled us only on basics. No kata or sparring, just basics, and some of them were brutal! In one drill, you faced your partner and kicked to the stomach area. Your partner would block your kick with his shin, and quickly return a kick. This went back and forth for what seemed hours. When we were through our shins would be full of lumps and bruises. If you didn't try to kick hard enough, Sensei would yell at you to kick faster and harder!

Sensei Kina would always do the drills with us, always picking a different student to practice with. We all prayed that he wouldn't pick us for his next victim. When he picked his daughters as his partner, he had no pity on them; he would kick them just as hard as everybody else, until tears would be rolling down their cheeks. They would never cry or give in.

This is just one of the many old drills he would have us do. Some of us still have scars to show from his brutal training. I would often think, "When are we going to learn kata? At least then we could get a little break!"

When we finally started to learn kata, Sensei Kina began with Kihon katas One and Two. These are the same katas Sensei Shoshin Nagamine called Fukyugata One and Two. Kata training was usually done in the last part of class. After we learned the section of Kihon One we were on, we would practice it over and over again every night. I don't remember exactly how long we stayed on Kihon One and Two, but for a while I thought it was going to be the only kata we would do. But after the two Kihons we moved on to the Pinan katas. Again, he drilled us on the Pinan katas until we could do them in our sleep! Sensei Kina was all about repetition, over and over, until we could do it without thinking. It was developing muscle memory, so every move was just reaction.

This is what karate is all about, reaction. Working every movement into the sub consciousness. React without thinking. The fight should be over in seconds. This is why repetition is so crucial. When training don't be afraid of the man who does five hundred different kinds of kicks. Be afraid of the man who does one kick five hundred times.

Eventually, Sensei Kina started teaching a few of us kobudo, beginning with the bo. We then moved on to the sai, tonfa, nunchuku and kama. The more kobudo he taught us, the more it would take away from our regular karate training, until he decided to have kobudo training on Wednesday nights only. At the end of each kobudo class, we would sit around in a circle and wipe down all our wooden weapons with old car oil that he brought from home, to saturate the wood and keep it from warping. There was usually always someone there that could translate what Sensei was saying. We would sit around, wiping down our weapons listening to him tell stories – and laugh our ass off. It was a great time.

I'd like to talk a bit about Sensei Masanobu Kina's early years in karate. The Kina family were originally from Shuri, and they go all the way back to King Sho Hashi. The head of the family held the title of *Pechin*, or scholar-official, who often served in administrative positions in the Ryukyuan government. The Kina family operated in secret as protectors of the Royal family. The Pechin were also trained in the martial arts.

Ebihara Isamu, senior Japanese student to Masanobu Kina and good friend to Robert Teller. Ebihara Sensei was from mainland Japan and would come two to three times a year to train with Masanobu Kina in Okinawa. Ebihara Sensei was a diligent teacher and outstanding gentleman who taught many lessons to author, who has nothing but his most profound respects. His untimely death was one that was sorely felt. His legacy is carried on at his dojo in mainland Japan by his senior student Keizo Nagira.

The oldest child of Shomo Kina, Masanobu Kina grew up in a household of thirteen people. His mother was just fourteen years old when he was born. Around the age of eight, he would watch every day as his Grandfather, Shojin Kina, and his grandfather's best friend, Shosei Kina, practiced martial arts behind their house. The two noticed how interested Masanobu was, and eventually asked him to join them. They were surprised at how fast he picked it up. The katas they taught were the family kata handed down to Shojin Kina, and a kata called *Shimabuku Passai*. Shosei Kina also taught the katas he learned from Kentsu Yabu. By the time Masanobu reached his teens, he had become an exceptionally good karate-ka.

Masanobu's father was a good friend of Chotoku Kyan. Shojin Kina and Shosei Kina suggested that Shomo to take Masanobu to train with Kyan. At first Sensei Kyan said no, he was too young, but after watching Masanobu train, he gave in and accepted him as a student. Masanobu Kina trained with Sensei Kyan until his late teens… and then World War II broke out. Like all young men his age, he was sent to mainland Japan and prepared for war.

After the war ended he returned to Okinawa, where he was accepted into the Okinawan police academy. The martial arts instructor at the academy was Chojun Miyagi, from whom he learned the basics of Gōjū-ryū. After graduating from the police academy he got a job on one of the American military bases. Some of the American security police witnessed him using his martial arts skills to settle a few incidents on base, and they were in awe! They asked him to teach them karate, but he refused. Even though he was working at a military base, he still considered the Americans his enemy.

After a while though, working side by side with the other American security police, he started to have a change of heart. They would eat lunch together every day and talk and laugh. Then one day when one of the Americans asked him again to teach them karate he finally agreed. They would meet after work on base and he soon had about twenty students. He did not speak much English and never got permission to teach on base. Eventually that became a problem because there were two other karate senseis teaching on base who did have written permission. Sensei Kina was told he could no longer teach on base.

When he told Father Ikehara what had happened, Father Ikehara suggested he teach at his church. He told his American students that they could continue their karate training at the church and in no time the class had doubled in size. Now they were getting Okinawan kids from the neighborhood and eventually some of their fathers joined. When the Vietnam War started some of his American students got orders to leave. They told Sensei Kina they would definitely be back to continue their karate training. He knew if they didn't come back, they were probably killed or injured. Sensei Kina would have his wife and daughters make a big meal for the departing students. They would drink sake infused with garlic, to make the soldiers more powerful, until they could barely walk out of his house. As they left he would tell them the Kina family would always be their family.

While Masanobu Kina was still a teen, he had begun studying the sai from his father's friend Shosei Kina. The sai kata *Ufuchiku no Sai* came from Shosei Kina. The young karate-ka fell in love with kobudo. He started learning the bo from a bo master named Oshiro Seiryu. He learned the kama from the famous Sensei Matsutaro Ire, who also was a good friend of the Kina family and lived nearby. The tonfa, sai and nunchaku kata which are practiced today were created by Masanobu Kina.

The empty-hand katas Masanobu Kina taught were mainly from Chotoku Kyan and from Sensei Yabu (through Shosei Kina). All were Shōrin-ryū. He didn't seem to like the Gōjū-ryū katas. Here is a list of the empty-hand katas he taught and the masters from whom he learned them:

Kihon I & II	*Nagamine sensei*
Pinon Katas	*Shosei Kina – Yabu Kentsu*
Naihanchi I, II, III	*Shosei Kina – Yabu Kentsu*
Kusanku Sho, Dai	*Shosei Kina – Yabu Kentsu*
Gojushiho	*Shosei Kina – Yabu Kentsu*
Passai	*Kyan Chotoku*
Chinto	*Kyan Chotoku*
Yara Chatan Kusanku	*Kyan Chotoku*
Wankan	*Kyan Chotoku*
Rohai	*Kyan Chotoku*
Wanshu	*Kyan Chotoku*
Ananku	*Kyan Chotoku*
Family kata	*Shojin Kina*
Shimabuku Passai	*Shosei Kina, Kazu Higa, Shimabuku, Nakamura, Soken, Matsumura*

As our dojo started to get better known around the area, we were often asked to put on demonstrations. One day an Air Force officer asked me if we could put on a demonstration on base. It would be at the base gym and a lot of people would be in attendance. A few days before the demonstration I asked Sensei Kina if he wanted to do the demonstration and he said "GOOD! OKAY!" in excitement. He then had me follow him to the home of a neighbor, who I later found out was head of one of the oldest families in his village.

When we got there we were invited into the house and Sensei Kina started talking to the gentleman in Japanese. Then the neighbor got up and walked over to the door, where a very old bo was hanging. It was only about five feet long and was black in color. The old man started to speak to me in English. He said Sensei Kina told him about this big karate demonstration on base. He wanted to use the family bo that was over one hundred and fifty years old. He said it meant a lot to Sensei Kina. When he told Sensei Kina he could use it, Sensei Kina was all smiles. I asked the gentlemen why was the bo was only five feet tall.

He said that a hundred years ago most Okinawans were under five foot tall and all the bos back then were shorter.

The demonstration was on a Saturday and the gym was packed. Sensei was finally up and you could tell he was excited. We told everybody in the gym about the weapon's history. He started to do his favorite bo kata… and halfway through he swung the bo so hard it snapped in two. It is impossible to describe the look on his face. He finished the kata with half of the bo, then ran off the floor and headed out the door.

I went outside after him and I thought he was going to throw up. There wasn't a sound in the gym. He got in my car and wanted to go home. Nothing was said all the way home. When we pulled up to his house I got out to open the door but he was already out. He was holding the two pieces of the bo in his hand and I said "I'll see you later, sensei." He started yelling something in Japanese, grabbed my arm and started pulling me behind him. Now I realized he was taking me with him back to the house where we got the bo! I'm thinking, "OH SHIT! ONE HUNDRED AND FIFTY YEARS OLD! A PRICELESS HEIRLOOM!"

He walked straight up to the door and knocked. When the door opened, Sensei Kina was standing there holding the two pieces of the broken bo. He started talking to the owner of the house in a very low voice with his head bowed down. The owner invited us into his house and started talking softly to Sensei Kina.

When he was finished talking to Sensei Kina, he looked at me and said, "I told your sensei not to worry, because I am going to glue the bo back together. I'm going to hang it back over the door and make a sign that reads, 'This bo was snapped in half by the famous karate master Masanobu Kina.'"

Sensei Kina and I both had tears in our eyes. We talked to the owner a little longer, and Sensei Kina seemed to feel a lot better. What an outstanding gentlemen the owner was!

THE BUNKASAI

Each year, every town and village holds a *bunkasai*, a celebration of a tradition that has been passed down over the years (dancing, singing, karate, etc.). Shimabuku village was looking forward to their *bunkasai*, and Masanoba Kina was put in charge. Because of his family background they decided to honor the three hundred Pechin, protectors of King Sho Hashi. Sensei Kina wanted all his students involved.

We trained almost every day for about a month before the festival. All the men from the village, young and old, would practice together. When the other Okinawans from the village found out he intended to let his American students participate, they were adamant: NO OUTSIDERS! Sensei angrily called a meeting. He told them they were still angry because of a war that ended over thirty years ago. He said that war was country against country, not person against person. He told them that they were being racist and he did not want to be any part of it. If his American students couldn't participate then he would not participate. "Find someone else to run your festival!" They took a vote and Sensei Kina won unanimously. We were the first non-Okinawans to ever participate in the bunkasai.

One day we were practicing bo for the bunkasai. Sensei Kina would drill us on basics over and over, and when everyone seemed to be able to handle his weapon properly, he started pairing us together. One of the drills we would do was combinations of striking to the head, then left side, right side, and upwards. We'd drill over and over; faster and faster, until we'd have to react without thinking. That's when I made my mistake. I started to think and lost the rhythm; I went up instead of down and got hit in the lip.

I felt the numbness on my lip right away, and when I tried to feel my lip with my tongue, it went through the gigantic hole right below my lip. My partner yelled and someone handed me a towel. We went to a phone and I called my wife to come and take me to the base hospital. I received about ten stitches, and they put a bandage on me and said to come back in a week. When we were driving home I said to my wife, "Let's stop back at the field where we were practicing, so I can tell Sensei I'm okay."

When I walked over to Sensei Kina and told him the outcome, he said "Good. Go get your bo!"

I said "YES SIR!" I got my bo and we practiced for about another half hour until it started to get dark.

The first group of Americans that performed at the Bunkasai with Master Masanobu Kina.

THE DEATH OF SENSEI MASANOBU KINA

As we progressed in our kobudo training, Sensei Kina started teaching us the first kama kata. It was called *Kobo Kama no Te*, but he just called it *Ire Kama*. As soon as we started to feel somewhat comfortable with the first kata, he started to teach us the second kama kata. This was not normal for him; it seemed like he just wanted to teach us all of his kata in a hurry, without perfecting one before moving on to the next. That was completely out of character. We had barely gotten through the tonfa kata when he started the kama kata.

I asked him politely if he would continue teaching more of the tonfa before we got into the kama. He looked at me with a hesitant look on his face, and then said okay. He started drilling us on the tonfa. Fighting with the tonfa, defending with the tonfa, tonfa against bo drills. It was great! Looking back, I believe he knew he was going to die. His grandfather had died at age 54 and his father died at the same age. He had just turned 54 and believed his end was near.

Then I got temporary orders to Korea for two weeks. After about a week in Korea, I decided to call my wife and see how she and the kids were doing. She was crying when she answered the phone, which frightened me.

"Did something happen to one of the kids?" I wondered?

"No, Sensei Kina just died, in a swimming accident looking for shells," she replied through her tears

I screamed, "NO, NO!" as I thought, "You can't die, Sensei! You have so much more to teach me!"

As soon as I got home, I went straight to Sensei Kina's house to pay my respects. As I looked at his picture and belongings in front of the shinza, I couldn't hold back my tears. When I said my goodbyes to the family, Sensei's wife came over to me and handed me his red and white obi.

I said "I can't take his belt from your family; it's a precious remembrance."

"No, he would have wanted you to have it," she replied.

Again with tears in my eyes, I accepted the belt, promising that I would never let anything happen to it, as long as I lived.

Now I had to decide what we would do with our dojo. Surely we couldn't let everything Sensei Kina worked so hard to create just die with him. Should we find another sensei who would take over our class and continue on?

Master Masanobu Kina's belt, along with the last sea shells he pick out of the ocean on the day of his death, adorns Robert Teller's shinza at his dojo. Belt and shells given to Robert Teller by sensei Kina's wife.

When I returned to work after Sensei Kina's death, I was sitting in my office in the Kadena medical emergency room. I was now the NCO in charge. I had an Okinawan ambulance driver named Satoshi Yamauchi, who was a senior black belt of Sensei Shian Toma. He would often come into my office when we weren't busy and we'd talk karate. He noticed that something was bothering me and asked me what was wrong. I told him about Sensei Kina, and that I didn't know what to do with the dojo.

Without hesitation he said, "Let me talk to Sensei Toma and ask him if he could take over the dojo."

A few months earlier, Sensei Kina and I had been invited to one of Sensei Toma's testing nights. Sensei Kina and Sensei Toma had talked, laughed and had a good time together. I know Sensei Kina really felt honored being invited by Sensei Toma. Sensei Toma's dojo was not that far from ours, and Sensei Yamauchi suggested that our students could go to Sensei Toma's dojo and train.

"That sounds great!" I said.

"Why don't you come with me tonight to sensei Toma's dojo and we can ask him together?" Yamauchi asked.

"Perfect! I'll meet you at Sensei Toma's dojo tonight."

When I got to Sensei Toma's dojo, Sensei Yamauchi was already there, explaining the situation. They called me over and Sensei Toma asked me questions about the dojo and the students. He told me he liked and respected Sensei Kina because he was very quiet and very humble. He said he would take over his dojo only if the Kina family agreed and we made plans to go to Sensei Kina's house.

A few days later, with Father Ikehara's help, we met with the Kina family. I had already spoken to them, so they knew of what the meeting was about. They agreed and were happy that our students could keep training. Before we left the house, Sensei Toma stated that would not start teaching for forty-nine days. He said that I would teach the class until then.

You may ask, "why forty-nine days?" When someone passes away in Okinawa, a funeral service usually occurs three to seven days after the death, followed by a ceremony on the forty-ninth day. Traditionally, the period of forty-nine days after someone dies is seen as a time for the deceased to check their consciousness and digest their karma. According to Buddhist tradition, the *bodhisattva* Ji Jang Bosal helps the deceased during these forty-nine days to perceive their karma so when they return, they are reborn to help this world, rather than continue in the cycle of birth and death.

A bodhisattva is one who dedicates their existence to helping others. Bodhisattva Ji Jang Bosal assists the deceased with their transition. Buddhism teaches that there is a life in this body, then a time of investigation or consideration, and then a new life in a new body. Even if you own a business and someone dies in your immediate family, you close the business for forty-nine days.

8

DR GORDON WARNER

During my time in Okinawa, I used to write for a local magazine called the *Okinawan Passtime*. It was geared toward GIs and had things like local places to visit, movie times and other information of use to Americans stationed on the island. I primarily wrote karate articles. One afternoon, I received a call from Barry Stier, the magazine's publisher. He said that Dr. Warner, also a writer for the magazine, wanted to meet me. Dr. Warner also did editing for Barry Stier and was one of the original writers for *Black Belt Magazine*. He also wrote extensively about the history of Okinawa, American generals in Okinawa, and many other historic articles. I was in shock! This man enjoyed presidential status on the island and I was very nervous at the idea of meeting him. When I asked Barry why Warner wanted to meet with me, he said he really liked my articles.

Our first meeting was over lunch. Dr. Warner asked me, "Are you doing any inter-views in the near future?" I told him I was; the following week I was scheduled to interview Sensei Shinyu Isa. He asked if he could come along to the interview. I said I would be honored. Little

The author with Dr. Warner and Master Shinyu Isa.

did I know at the time that I was about to get a lesson on how to do professional interviews from one of the best.

We met the following week and headed over to sensei Isa's dojo. When we arrived I approached the anteroom of the dojo and started to take off my *zori* (Japanese shoes). Dr. Warner placed his hand on my shoulder and showed me the traditional way of removing my shoes before entering a dojo. This was the first of many lessons I gratefully learned from Dr. Warner.

When we entered the dojo and Sensei Isa saw Dr. Warner, he looked shocked. He called the dojo to attention, and everyone – including Sensei Isa – bowed to Dr. Warner. They were awestruck at his presence at the dojo, and of course I felt very special, having brought him. After the interview, out of respect for Dr. Warner, Sensei Isa gave a demonstration that was beyond anything I had ever seen him do. If you ever get a chance to read the biography of Dr. Gordon Warner, a Marine who was considered for the Congressional Medal of Honor, you won't regret it.

A SHORT SYNOPSIS OF HIS BIOGRAGHY

This was provided to me by his children; daughter Irene Tomoe Cooper and son Ion Masashi Warner.

Dr. Gordon Warner was born on the twenty-fourth of October 1912 in Long Beach California. He joined the United State Marine Corps 24 May 1935 and reported to Marine Corps Recruit Depot, San Diego California. He was an honor graduate of the 1st Platoon Leaders Class and was commissioned a second lieutenant 7 July 1936.

After attending The Basic School at Philadelphia Navy Yard, he was transferred to the Marine Corps Reserve. In 1941, then 1st Lt. Warner joined the 1st Marine Raider Battalion, and later transferred to USMC Recruit Barracks San Diego, for duty as the commanding officer of Sea School. He was later assigned as commanding officer at Reserve Officer's Training School, Green Farm, San Diego.

He was ordered to the Special Weapons Battalion, 3rd Marine Division, Camp Elliot, San Diego. He deployed with 3rd Marine

Division to Auckland, New Zealand, and later fought with 3rd Marine Division Expeditionary Force at Guadalcanal. He organized and led a five-man patrol on a fifteen-day reconnaissance mission with Australian Coast Watchers behind Japanese lines, on Choiseul Island. Upon his return he was cited by Lt. Col. Arthur Trench, AIF, Australian Resident Commissioner.

On November 1, 1943, as commanding officer of Bravo Company, 3rd Regiment, he led the initial wave landing on Cape Torokina, Island of Bougainville, and was later awarded the Navy Cross for his actions. He was ordered to take Bravo Company to the left perimeter and stop a thousand-strong Japanese landing force conducting a left flank push against Col. Cragi's 9th Marines.

The firefight began at 0600 and raged all day long, with Dr. Warner's company finally overrunning the Japanese opposition. Dr. Warner used his Japanese language skills to help win the fight by confusing the enemy, yelling false orders to those close enough to hear him. Toward the end of the battle, Dr. Warner had taken command of a tank and led it into a clearing, where it came under heavy fire from two Japanese machine gun nests.

The tank took many hits, one of which penetrated the tank's armor and hit Dr. Warner in the left leg, shattering the bone. Dr. Warner was awarded the Navy Cross for taking out the machine gun nest and was recommended for the Medal of Honor for his actions that day. Due to the serious injury he sustained, Dr. Warner lost his left leg, amputated just below the hip (leaving only approximately six inches of his femur remaining), and subsequently spent quite a while recovering in the hospital. His decorations also include the Purple Heart and an Australian Citation.

Dr. Warner received one of the highest citations of the Department of Army, The Patriotic Civilian Service Award. He served as Chief "A" Veterans Guidance Center, U.S. Veteran Administration, Regional Office, Los Angeles. He later served as the director of the Education Department, Ryukyu Islands, and Advisor to the High Commissioner of the Ryukyu Islands. He retired from the U.S. Federal Civil Service in

1978. In 2001 Dr. Warner was awarded The Order of the Sacred Treasure, Gold Rays with Neck Ribbon, by the Emperor of Japan for his significant contributions to Japan and his leadership in Japanese martial arts.

As a tireless steward to learning, Dr. Warner served as an instructor at Punahou Academy, Honolulu; Honolulu Police Department, Maui High School, Los Angeles City College, Oakland, California Public Schools, University of California Berkley, and California State University, Long Beach. Academic assignments included serving as visiting Professor, Tokyo National University and teaching thirty-one years with the University of Maryland, Far East and Asian Divisions. He has lectured in Taiwan, South Korea and throughout Japan.

Dr. Warner conducted research and lectured on the Okinawan War in Brussels, Switzerland, Greece, Egypt, India, Hong Kong, Hawaii, Australia and UK. He also authored several books on the Okinawa War, Japanese martial arts, Japanese festival and Japanese chopsticks.

Academic accomplishments included: a B.S. and M.S. in Communications, an M.A. in history and a Ph.D., all from the University of Southern California (USC), as well as an Ed.D. in International Education from University of California, Berkley.

Dr. Warner would eventually take up residence in Okinawa, Japan, where he would spend the rest of his days. During his time in Okinawa and mainland Japan, Dr. Warner decided to continue his training in the art of kendo, which he had started while a student at the University of Southern California. Dr. Warner participated in many *shiai*, such as the All-Japan High School and University Teacher's tournament and the All-Japan Medical Doctor's tournament, even winning some of his matches. Much to his delight people would remark on his excellent technique and not his handicap. Dr. Warner obtained the rank of Kyoshi 7th dan in kendo and 6th dan in Iaido. Remarkably Dr. Warner achieved all of this without the use of his left leg.

Dr. Warner passed away at age ninety-seven and is interred at Arlington National Cemetery. He is survived by daughter Irene Tomoe Cooper, son Ion Masashi Warner and two grandchildren.

9
SHIAN TOMA

It was 1978 when we asked Sensei Toma to take over Sensei Kina's class. At that time, he was still the senior student to Master Uehara of Motobu-ryū. Short in stature but sturdily built and strong as an ox, he had Popeye-like forearms and hands like an iron vice. Many students learned just how strong he was during toide lessons, when he tossed men twice his size around like rag dolls. Unlike many of the old Okinawan masters, who either outright refused to teach Americans or only shared a small part of karate with them, Sensei Toma held very different beliefs.

While he had lived through the horrors of World War II, he also worked for many years on Kadena as a flight-line bus driver, and got to know a lot of Americans personally. This probably influenced his relationship with the GIs as people, rather than just karate students and an extra source of income. He was one of the few Okinawan sensei who I know that never hesitated to teach Americans.

Master Shian Toma and Robert Teller at the nursing home shortly after Master Masanobu Kina's death

Right before Sensei Toma was to start teaching at Kina's dojo, which at that time was still at the nursing home, I went out and had a sign made that read: *OKINAWAN MOTOBU RYU*. I put it in cement out by the road to attract more students. The first day Sensei Toma came to teach, I proudly showed him the sign; I thought he was going to be happy, but he angrily told me to take it down. That sign cost me a lot of money, but when I saw the look on his face, I couldn't get it down fast enough!

I didn't know it at the time, but American students and outsiders were not accepted in Master Uehara's system. He let Americans study at Sensei Toma's dojo, but with the understanding that he would not teach us the true *Motobu-ryū Undun Di* art. We were not allowed to participate at any Motobu functions, and what we thought was Motobu-ryū toide, was actually basic *akijitsu*. This would eventually bother Sensei Toma and once he had the opportunity, he did things his way.

After a few months training at the nursing home, and because of the differences between Sensei Kina's and Sensei Toma's systems, many students stopped training. Those of us that stayed with

Satoshi Yamauchi being thrown by Grandmaster Shian Toma

Sensei Toma started attending class at his main dojo, which sat just off Kadena in a small unassuming building off *Kuko Dori* (Gate Street).

This is when I first met Sensei Shigemitsu Tamae. Sensei Tamae was Sensei Toma's senior student and I was blown away at his speed and power. He was a national competitor, captain of his college karate club in mainland Japan, and a world karate champion. Sensei Tamae became a renowned and much feared fighter in the Motobu-ryū system.

Back in those days in Okinawa, just like the old West gun fighters in America, great kumite fighters were often challenged. Word would spread about a talented fighter, and would-be challengers would come seek him out. They'd often show up at Sensei Uehara's dojo, because of his student's reputation as being the best fighters on Okinawa. Sensei Tamae was always assigned to meet the challenge, and legend has it that he never lost a fight.

Sometime in the Seventies, Uehara Sensei started conducting the all Motobu-ryū karate and kobudo championships, and Sensei Toma wanted his American students to participate. At that point, we had some really good Gaijin fighters thanks to Sensei Toma and Tamae's hard training. When he approached Sensei Uehara and asked permission for his American students to compete, one of Sensei Uehara's Okinawan black belts jumped in and said in no uncertain terms "NO AMERICANS!"

Sensei Uehara looked at Sensei Toma, paused, nodded and repeated, "No Americans."

Sensei Toma looked at the black belt who had said spoken up, gave him the look of death and then walked out of the dojo. I'd seen that look on Sensei Toma's face on a few past occasions and believe me, you didn't want to be the focus of it. The look was sent in my direction only once and it would shake you down to your very soul. Sensei was a great man but you did not want to get on his bad side. That story was told to me by one of Sensei Toma's senior black belts who had been there.

Shortly after that incident and after a lot of soul searching, Sensei Toma met with Uehara Sensei and told him he was leaving Motobu-ryū. They parted on good terms and remained friends. One night after training, Sensei Toma called his senior students together and told us we were no longer Motobu-ryū; our style was now to be called Seidokan.

"Seidokan Shorin Ryu?" I asked.

"NO! Just Seidokan!" he replied.

Letting my mouth get in front of my brain (as usual), I asked "Don't we have to have a ryu?"

"NO, just like Shotokan."

Sensei Toma had originally called his dojo simply "Toma Dojo," then Seidokan, which interpreted into English means "A House of the

True Way." That meaning is often misinterpreted by some Seidokan practitioners as "THE House of the True Way." Sensei Toma, however, would never be so presumptuous to believe that his way was the only true way. That just wasn't his style, evidenced by his encouraging his students to study with other karate masters on the island.

Seidokan was to be a mix of all the karate Sensei Toma had learned in his life; the katas of Shōrin-ryū, the wrist locks of Motobu-ryū and the various kobudo he had learned. An interesting story of the development of Seidokan was Sensei Toma's *Toma no Kama* kata. He had been studying with an Okinawan master named Sensei Ire, who was known for his kama kobudo. Sensei Toma would train with him once a week to learn the kama kobudo but it would change every week. Eventually, he realized that Sensei Ire was going senile and had forgotten what he has already taught. Sensei Toma decided to take the beginning of a kata he had learned from Sensei Ire and finished it on his own, turning it into *Toma no Kama*.

When my wife and I were first married, I didn't have two nickels to rub together, and we really didn't have much of a wedding. Years later, when I was much more financially stable, we decided to do it right and went to a wedding photographer off-base, who did a series of portraits of us in traditional Okinawan garb. Sensei Toma really liked the pictures so I asked him if he wanted to do some photos with the same photographer. He got very excited about the prospect, so one morning I brought him down to the same photographer. The photos came out fantastic and one of them has been used in Seidokan dojos all over the world.

During much of the time I was studying with Sensei Toma, I was writing for the *Okinawan Passtime* magazine. My articles were called "Karate Close-up."

My first interview for the magazine was with Sensei Nagamine of Matsubayashi-Ryū, then Sensei Uechi of Uechi-Ryū, and Sensei Yagi from Goju-Ryū. After these three masters, I went to Sensei Toma and nervously asked if he could arrange an interview with Sensei Uehara. At that time, I didn't know what their relationship was after the split. He said he would talk with him and eventually arranged the requested interview.

When we arrived on a Friday evening I was surprised at how friendly Sensei Uehara and Sensei Toma were to each other. They talked, laughed and really seemed to enjoy one another's company. I remember when Sensei Uehara entered the room, he was still wearing his Karate gi and his hair was silver and combed straight back. When he walked it was with a military bearing, his back straight and looking like a man twenty years younger. He was about seventy-six years old at the time. I was in awe that I finally met the famous Master Uehara. The only other karate master that gave me this kind of feeling was Master Hohan Soken. They were both what I consider a master's master!

Master Uehara was very polite to me and answered all my questions. He was much older than Sensei Toma, and I learned he had fought in the Japanese army in China. Knowing that we were once his enemy, I stayed away from any questions about the war. I was surprised to find out that he had also trained with other prominent Okinawan karate masters. I was under the impression that he had only studied in the *Motobu-Ryū Undun Di* system. Based on his answers, I gleaned that he only trained with these other prominent martial artists to learn their fighting techniques. I believe that this interview with Sensei Uehara was one of my best and most insightful.

His story reminded me of the Okinawan legend of Chinto, a famous Chinese martial artist and pirate who was one the most famous kung-fu practitioners of his day. The story goes that his ship washed up on the shores of Okinawa during a storm and they remained on the island for many days. Word got around that this famous kung-fu pirate was training down on the beach, and Bushi Matsumura, one of the Okinawan king's Pechin, decided to go meet him. He took food and drink down to where Chinto was staying and the two men became quick friends.

Never mentioning his own karate training, Bushi Matsumura told Chinto that he heard that he was an expert in the martial arts. Chinto acknowledged that he studied kung-fu and Matsumura asked if the pirate would teach him some. Chinto agreed and they began meeting and practicing down on the beach every day. Bushi Matsumura's main objective was to learn Chinto's techniques and make them his own. Under the veil of hospitality, he managed to determine the pirate's skill level and technique. This would make it easier to force him off the island if it became necessary. Legend tells us that the kata called Chinto, practiced in many systems to this day, was passed down from this encounter.

The martial arts world is not immune to gossip and jealousy, and apparently another karate teacher from Okinawa City with the same last name, Seiki Toma, claimed that Shian Toma had been his student. When I interviewed Sensei Shian Toma a few months later for the magazine article, I thought this would be the perfect time to set the story straight. I asked Sensei Toma about this, he was emphatic that he had NEVER been a student of Seiki Toma. I could tell that this bothered him and I quickly dropped the subject. Even years later, Seiki Toma's biography on some websites state that Sensei Toma was one of his students, but I've known the truth for decades, though I always wished Sensei Toma would have given me a bit more than his terse response.

After my last tour of duty on Okinawa ended in 1981, I received orders back to the United States. I had been lucky enough to experience a total of three tours of duty on Okinawa. Each one I had voluntarily extended the length of my tour. When I told Sensei Toma that I was returning to the States for good (though I would visit), he said he would like to talk to me after class.

We went to a local Okinawan bar not far from the dojo to talk. Sensei Toma told me he would like me to open a Seidokan dojo. I was being assigned to Pottstown Pennsylvania as an Air Force recruiter. I knew I'd have time to teach, so I agreed. When I got settled in, I opened my first Seidokan dojo in the basement of a VFW post. It grew quickly, and before I knew it, we out grew the new building. We had to move to a larger facility and I was lucky to have committed students who were hungry to learn. I taught traditional Okinawan karate exactly like I had learned in Okinawa. NO COMMERCIAL KARATE that handed out belts like candy on Halloween! We didn't go to many tournaments but when we did, most of the students would usually return with a trophy.

Shiai with Bruce Heilman's dojo and the author's dojo 1981. Robert Teller's students in attendance were: Jody Paul, Bob Boback, Bob Trotta, Wayne Benfield, Chris Caggiano, Steve Barnes, Bob Wright, Lee Stowe, Loretta Cappaletti, and Mark Himmel

Every year or two my wife and I would return to Okinawa to visit family. I would train with sensei Toma whenever I could. Sensei Toma would always invite me his special Black belt training on Saturday nights. I was the only non-Okinawan. This training was completely different than any other training I had done before. I'd get home from that training and could barely stand up or hold a fork in my hand.

After four or five years teaching in the States, I decided to invite Sensei Toma and Sensei Tamae to come to my school. My thought was to have an all Seidokan seminar and tournament. I believed it would be a good time to get all the Seidokan members from all over the world together so Sensei Toma could reorganize and structure Seidokan the way he wanted it to run. It was a great success, with attendees from the United States, Great Britain, Spain and Italy.

10
TAIKA SEIYU OYATA

One afternoon in the late Eighties, I was working out in my dojo when a stranger came in. He said his name was Dale Knepp and he was a student of Sensei Seiyu Oyata. He lived in Missouri and was home visiting his family in Pennsylvania, not far from my karate school. I had heard Sensei Toma talk about Sensei Oyata, but until that time I didn't know too much about him. Dale said that Sensei Oyata and Sensei Toma were good friends. When Sensei Oyata heard that Dale was going home to Pennsylvania, he asked him to see if he could find my dojo. Dale and I worked out for a while, and when he had to leave he said he was going to ask Greg Lindquist, one of Sensei Oyata's senior students, to call me.

Taika Seiyu Oyata and author Robert Teller

A few days later I received a call from Greg. We talked for a while and then he said that Sensei Oyata wanted to talk to me. OH SHIT! I broke out in a cold sweat and told him I'll get my wife and they can talk in their Okinawan dialect.

When she got on the phone, she laughed a lot and must have talked to sensei Oyata for half hour. My wife hung up the phone and I asked if Sensei Oyata wanted to talk to me. She laughed and said, "No, he'd like to come visit us and maybe have a seminar. She said that Greg Lindquist would call me to discuss if it would be possible.

Greg called me the next day; we discussed Sensei Oyata's plans for a seminar and I agreed. We arranged for him to come the following month. When he arrived as scheduled on Friday morning, my wife had been excitedly cooking for two days, all of the Okinawan favorites he requested. We all sat at the kitchen table and laughed, told stories and became friends. By the end of that first day he jokingly had claimed my wife as his daughter. I like to think he considered our home his home.

Friday night I had arranged for our students to show Sensei Oyata our dojo and do a short demo. At this time my dojo was behind my home. I put a big comfortable chair in the front of the dojo for Sensei Oyata to sit in and watch. After about two minutes into our demo, Sensei Oyata stood up and told us to sit down. He got in the middle of our dojo floor, still in his street clothes, and began throwing our black belts around like rag dolls! He was doing things that I had heard of but had never seen before. This was the "real" traditional Okinawan karate that was kept secret from American karateka and ALL non-Okinawan karateka. Everyone in the room, their mouths agape, were in awe. We had never seen anything like it before.

The author's autographed photo of Taika Seiyu Oyata.

As the night went on, Sensei Oyata's students from all over the country started dropping in unexpectedly. The demo turned into a workout and eventually a big party. I was afraid that no one would be able to show up for the real seminar the next morning.

After several training sessions and seminars with Taika Oyata, I decided that I wanted my two boys to be able to train with a real Okinawan karate master. Since Sensei Oyata lived in the United States we would be able to train with him much more frequently than going to Okinawa once a year. The next day my wife called Sensei Toma and explained our situation to him and why we would like to train with Sensei Oyata. Sensei Toma said that he understood and that he was good friends with Sensei Oyata and wished us the best.

In my view, Sensei Oyata is one of the greatest physical karate practitioners I ever saw. There are many stories about other great Okinawan masters but I never saw them with my own eyes. I can only talk about those that I have actually seen, and during my time in Okinawa I was blessed to have witnessed many.

There are so many great memories of Taika Oyata, but I'd like to share a few of my fondest.

Master Oyata would usually come to our house two or three times a year. The first time he visited our dojo we had a full schedule. We trained all day Friday, then that night he gave a *tanbo* (short staff) seminar for the kids. Saturday was an all-day seminar at Villanova University. After the seminar we took Taika out to eat.

Dinner after Taika Oyata seminar hosted by Robert Teller

It was a lot of eating, drinking and laughing, and when we got home late on Saturday night, Taika, exhausted, went straight to bed. He was staying in my son's bedroom, which was right next to our master bedroom. The bathroom was directly across from both rooms. Taika got up at around 3 o'clock in the morning to use the bathroom. Half asleep, he came out of the bathroom and instead of turning left to go into his room, he turned right, straight into our bedroom. Miko was sleeping closest to the door, and Taika jumped into bed where Miko was sleeping. I was on the far side, sound asleep, and was awoken by a loud shriek. The first scream came from Sensei Oyata and the next was from my wife. I had to laugh because that night Taika screamed louder than my wife!

The second memory was when my wife and I drove to the airport to pick up Sensei Oyata. He would be very adamant about people being punctual and waiting for him as he came off the plane. About two miles from the airport on I-95 my car died, but luckily we managed to coast to the side of the highway. I tried to start the car, but to no avail; it was as dead as can be. Some people stopped to try and help us, but no one could get the car started. I looked at my watch and realized that Taika Oyata's plane was landing and we were still two miles away from the airport with no car.

Another passerby stopped to offer help. I asked him if there was any way he could take my wife and drop her off at the airport and he happily obliged. By the time my wife got to the airport Taika's plane had been on the ground for about an hour. When she finally found him, he was not happy and made sure she knew it. There was a lot of *Uchinaguchi*, being said at the time. My wife said whenever Taika would get upset with her, he would speak in native Okinawan.

They then got a taxi and came back to my car. I had called AAA so they could take my car to my local garage. Luckily Miko and Taika arrived at the same time AAA did. I got in the taxi and we headed to Enterprise Car Rental to get a car for the weekend. It was rush hour and it couldn't have happened at a worse time!

When we finally got home, Miko ran to the kitchen to warm things up so Taika could have a nice dinner. When she went to turn the electric cook top stove on, it wouldn't work. Taika asked what was wrong when Miko yelled. She told him the stove wasn't working. He walked into the kitchen and tried to fix it. After about fifteen minutes he came out and said "Stove no good."

Taika Oyata and Robert Teller working out in his home dojo on bo staff disarms

When we finally got home, Miko ran to the kitchen to warm things up so Taika could have a nice dinner. When she went to turn the electric cook top stove on, it wouldn't work. Taika asked what was wrong when Miko yelled. She told him the stove wasn't working. He walked into the kitchen and tried to fix it. After about fifteen minutes he came out and said "Stove no good."

I told him I would run to Sears and get a new cook top and was back within an hour. We took the cook top stove out of the box and when Taika and I went to put it in the old opening it wouldn't fit. He asked me if I had a circular saw. I got one and he then went to town sawing away at my cabinet. Then he hooked up all of the wiring, allowing Miko to complete her cooking. I kept apologizing over and over again to Taika for the inconvenience, to which he finally replied, "Shut up, let's eat." We all broke out in laughter. It couldn't have been a worse day!

By Sunday I had gotten my car back from the garage, but Taika refused to be driven back to the airport with me and my "unreliable" car. I ended up getting Taika back to the airport with one of his black belts, and my good friend Jim Toolan.

The third memory was when Taika came to my dojo one Friday afternoon. He would always fly into Philadelphia International Airport. However, on this trip we got super cheap tickets, but the flight flew into

Lehigh Valley International Airport, near Allentown; an airport I was not familiar with. After Taika got into my car, I got back on the main highway that ran in front of the Airport. Right away I started talking to sensei Oyata about karate. Whenever I was alone with him I would drill him about his early years in karate.

We talked and talked and then it hit me, we had been driving on this highway for over thirty minutes. I was only on this highway for five or ten minutes coming to the airport. Then I realized I was heading in the wrong direction; we were in New Jersey instead of Pennsylvania. I was lost and didn't know where the hell I was! What should have taken forty to fifty minutes took us over two hours! My wife started calling me and wanted to know where I was. She had Sensei's dinner ready, and reminded me that we were having testing at my dojo at six pm! I can't repeat what Taika said; suffice it to say he was not pleased.

That night at testing, Taika sat with me in the front of the class. One of the first to come up to test was a little boy. He did his kata and he looked pretty good. Taika asked the boy how often he practiced (meaning at home). The little boy replied, "Every Tuesday and Thursday from six to seven pm, at the karate school." Everybody, including Taika, started laughing. Taika got up and walked over to the little boy. He put his hand on the boy's shoulder and faced all of the parents. He said that young children are very honest and usually always tell the truth. But sometimes, children learn at home not to always tell the truth. For example, if the phone rings and it's for one of the parents, the parent might tell the child, "Tell them I'm asleep." They are teaching their children to lie.

He continued and told the room that we have to be careful of what we say and do around our children. Everyone stood up and applauded him. With tears in my eyes, I thought right then and there that there's so much more to karate then just punching and kicking. How lucky I have been over the years to have had such great karate masters.

The next to come up and do his kata in front of Taika was an adult student. I thought his kata was pretty sharp. I learned over and whispered in Taika's ear, "What did you think of his kata?" He turned to me and calmly said, "I killed him ten times."

My jaw dropped. "WHAT?" I said.

He replied that when he watched their kata, he fights them in his head. If their face was open, he knocked them out! If their groin was left open, he kicked them in the groin! When you do kata, you have to be thinking defense and protecting your body at all times. You always think defense before offence and eventually it will become one. I smiled and shook my head in approval. My day went from horrible to great; Taika said that whenever you learn something, it's like putting a gold nugget in your money pouch! That night I put two gold nuggets in my pouch.

The fourth and final memory I would like to talk about, is when my good friend John Snyder had sensei Odo at his dojo. John's dojo was about forty-five minutes away from ours. Sensei Oyata was at my dojo.

Both teachers had been training partners with Sensei Nakamura of Okinawan Kenpo years earlier. I thought it would be a great idea if we could get both teachers together since they hadn't seen each other in a long time. I called John Snyder and told him of my idea. He said that would be GREAT! Why don't you bring Taika Oyata

Taika Oyata, Sensei Seikichi Odo, and the author at the banquet

and all his students up here? He said that they were having a banquet and we could surprise both teachers.

When we arrived both sensei were surprised and excited! Sensei Odo ran out and put on his karate gi. When he came back, he got out on the floor in front of everybody. He did an empty hand kata and a weapons kata. Like only sensei Odo could do! THEN, not to be over shadowed, Taika Oyata got on the floor in his civilian clothes. He started with self-defense techniques, which led to a few knock out techniques, using his own students! After the two Grandmasters were done, other high ranking black belts also did kata. Great banquet and a great night! Both sensei sat, ate together and reminisced about old times. A night I will never forget!

An interesting story of both Sensei's Oyata and Toma was that they were contemporaries in Okinawa and at one time rivals. As young men, they had an epic fight where both men emerged bloodied, bruised and friends for life. Having heard that story, I once had an opportunity to show Sensei Toma a video I had taken during a seminar of Oyata doing his famous knockouts. I asked Sensei Toma what he thought and he shrugged and said calmly "last man standing wins."

Taika Oyata and a student just moments after knocking him out to the floor.

In 2012, I lost my friend, my karate master, and for the first time in over fifty years, my karate link to Okinawa. Taika Oyata was bigger than life, and when we lost him, we couldn't believe – and still can't believe – that he is really gone. If we had a question about anything we could pick up the phone and call him. Whether it be a karate question or a personal problem, it didn't matter; he would always listen and always have an answer. Not always what we wanted to hear, but almost always the right answer.

His death hit us all in different ways. For me it was the first time in my karate life that I didn't have an Okinawan karate master. Master Shian Toma died almost a year later.

Who would I learn from, who would be able to answer all the technical karate questions that always pop up in my head? How would I get my promotion to 8th dan, or for that matter, any other karate promotions? The year Sensei Oyata died, eight of us had been told we would be tested for 8th dan. This may sound very selfish of me but it bothered me very much.

I started to think about all the one-on-one talks we had when Taika Oyata stayed at my house for a seminar. It was usually around two o'clock in the morning, after the last students had gone. He and I would be finishing up what was left of the sake and Okinawan food my wife had prepared. That was when I would learn the most from him. I remember one night asking him, "What will happen to our association when you die? Shouldn't we have an Okinawan student learn your system and keep it alive in Okinawa? Can we bring someone from Okinawa so you can train him and keep your roots in your home land? What will happen to your American students?"

I still remember the look on his face when I asked him the first question. Keeping the roots in Okinawa? He paused for a while looking down at the table and then said to me, "The older students like yourself who have been studying a long time will probably do what I and a lot of the other senior student did when Nakamura Sensei died. You take what you learned from me and from your other Okinawan instructors and try to take it to the next level!" He never answered my first question.

Around a year after he died, my wife and I went to Okinawa for our first vacation after my recent retirement. We stayed with my wife's younger sister, Akemi, and my brother-in-law, Ronnie Nix, who had by then achieved 9th dan under Sensei Toma. My older son Jimmy and two of my senior black belts accompanied us.

A few days after we got there, Akemi asked us if we would like to go sightseeing since it was the first time on Okinawa for my two black belts. Of course, we all said yes, and a couple of her karate students joined us. We learned that Sensei Tetsuhiro Hokama had invited us to his Gōjū-ryū dojo and Okinawan Karate museum. He would then take us on a karate sightseeing tour of Shuri and Naha cities.

As we toured Sensei Hokama's dojo and museum, the first thing we saw was a picture of Taika Oyata, and a group picture of Taika Oyata's students. They had visited Sensei Hokama's dojo on a trip to Okinawa. Sensei Hokama told us that for years Oyata always came to his dojo to train together when he was in Okinawa. Sensei Hokama said he was amazed at Oyata's toide, and had never seen anything like it on Okinawa. Then came the big shocker; he said that Sensei Oyata had promoted him to 10th Dan in 2004; the group pictures that was hanging on his wall was from that promotion.

As soon as I got back to the States, I made phone calls to some of the students in the picture; they corroborated that Sensei Oyata had promoted Sensei Hokama to 10th Dan. That brought back the memories of the early morning talk we had in my dining room. Was this Taika Oyata's way of keeping his roots in Okinawa?

About a week after our meeting with Sensei Hokama, Akemi invited him to her home for dinner. After dinner, my wife asked Sensei Hokama what happens in the Okinawan karate schools when the teacher dies. How do the higher ranked students get promoted? His answer was that some 8th, 9th and all 10th degrees are usually given rank from other organizations, such as the *Okinawan Times* newspaper and other big corporations on the island. These ranks are not given out for physical abilities, but for what the student has given back to karate and the spread of Okinawan culture. There are many other Okinawan and Japanese karate organizations made up of different karate styles that also promote higher ranks in different systems, such as the All Okinawan Karate Kobudo Rengokai and the Japanese Dai Nippon Butokukai.

When my wife told him I was scheduled to test for 8th dan the same year Sensei Oyata died, Sensei Hokama said "Sensei Oyata promoted me to 10th dan and I will promote your husband to 8th." Ronnie Nix later told Shigemitsu Tamae Sensei (at that point, the new headmaster of Seidokan) what Hokama Sensei was going to do. He said that was a good idea and said he would also like to be a part of the promotion, as I had been with Seidokan for many years under its founder. Then, five years later, February of 2017, I received the rank of 9th dan from Sensei Hokama.

One thing I would like to say about legitimate karate rank promotion. There are a lot of unscrupulous karate practitioners who try to sell rank for ridiculous testing fees. Most of these so-called karate "masters" bought their own rank. If you have any morals, stay away from these people. There are a number of good, legitimate karate organizations in the U.S. that issue true rank.

All my karate certificates hanging on my dojo wall are from my Okinawan karate senseis, with legitimate time in grade. Thanks to Masters Tetsuhiro Hokama and Shigemitsu Tamae, I still have two great masters to learn from, and ask all the technical karate questions that pop into my head. Even more important to me, I still have my karate roots in Okinawa! As of the publishing of this book, I will be seventy-two years old with fifty-three years in Okinawan karate.

Taika Seiyu Oyata, I miss you dearly and may you forever rest in peace. Till we meet again!

11

THE WRAP UP

So that's my journey so far. It is far from over, but I am well along the path that I first set out on over fifty years ago. There were some difficult challenges along the way, and I anticipate there will be more challenges as I continue. I am happy though with the road I chose, and every challenge has only made me stronger.

I know that some of you, my readers, have gone through some of these same struggles and more. Some of you, however, may still be in the first steps of your journey. To the latter, I give this advice. Be warned: when I first got my black belt I thought I had arrived, now that I was a black belt I could do anything! I soon got over it. There are many who don't.

Black belt means only that you have mastered the fundamentals sufficiently that you can start to learn the art. However, there are first- and second-degree black belts who believe their black belt means they are experts; they leave their sensei and open schools. Then they get together with other low-level black belts, form an association, and award each other higher and higher rank. They use slick marketing to attract students. They give out rank like Halloween candy – but they themselves have learned only the bare fundamentals, and you can't teach what you don't know. Believe me, there is no such thing as a legitimate thirty-five year-olds 10th degree!

If all you want is a black belt – or even a high ranking black belt – there are schools that will take your money and award you rank. I've even seen some web sites that promise to make you a black belt over the Internet. Don't believe it – a belt and a certificate do not an expert make! If you want to earn a black belt that has meaning, you have to take the journey.

My road spanned more than a half-century, and sometimes I didn't think I could go on. Looking back now, it seems like the time flew by – sometimes it seems like months rather than years – and I cherish every bruise, every bloody nose and every broken bone like gold and diamonds, because every single one made me stronger. I know my journey has no end, but neither is there any end to its value!

Ganbatte kudasai, fellow journeyer!

Robert Teller's first black belt on the left 1 ¼ inches wide compared to the present day belt which is 1 ¾ inches wide. (I won't tell you the length difference!)

My life started with Okinawan Karate and it will end with Okinawan Karate.

祝 囚 清勇 Presented to Miko Teller by Seiyu Oyata Jan. 1993

Okinawan dance has a long and dignified history, going back many centuries. It is a cultural treasure, having been passed down, with little change over time from master to student. The training of dancers is difficult and exacting, much like training in "Martial Arts". These dances are part of Okinawan folklore and tell stories that are tragic, funny, or mythical. During certain periods of Okinawan history, especially when the country was occupied by a foreign power, Karate Masters practiced these dances and included martial techniques hidden in their movements.

Mrs. Teller began her training as a dancer when she was six years old under "Higa Ryotoko" of Miyagi Ryu. Later, she was a disciple of "Hamamoto", a woman then in her sixties who taught into her nineties. Additionally, Mrs. Teller has extensive training in the "Martial Arts". She has danced professionally for many years in Okinawa and Japan, once with "Hohan Sohen".

Mrs. Teller has been fortunate to have received instruction from "Taka Oyata" who has helped her immensely with her techniques and has polished her Naginata skills.

We in America are fortunate to have an artist like Miko Teller touching our lives.

琉歌

父の好きだった琉歌に私の想いをのせて

けふのほこらしやなおにぎやなたてる
親子振合はちゃるけふの嬉しさや
つぼでをる花の露きやたごと

昨年ロバートさん靖子さん、二え先生、明天先生が父の仏壇に手を合わせたいと家を探し訪ねてくださいました。その日の嬉しさに何ともてなす事もできず申し訳なく思っていました。
そして昨度、父の為に本を出版すると申し出てくださり来てくださいました。そして真実と疑問に思っている事を子以上に父を愛し敬い、父の遺した足跡を懸命に探し求めるロバートさんの姿勢に私達ができる事は、ただ、父と過ごした日々を思い起こし忠実に伝える事だと思いました。
松田自身もあまりにも突然の別れにそくなった事を受け止める事ができずにいました。傷ついた心は仲々癒えずにいましたが、そんな時に海尾原さんの道えをつぐ、なぎらさんに空手の聖を伝授するロバートさんの姿に父の姿が重なりました。
父がいつも話していた、アメリカで空手を広めると言う言葉通り、ロバートさんと一緒に空手を広めると言う比嘉先生を父がいつも一緒にいるんだと思い思慕です。

とくし

休んでいた空手人生を私の中にいる父と比嘉先生と一緒にもう一度歩み続けようと思いました。
結びに
言葉では言いつくせない感謝とこれからの私を導きそさだいましたロバートさん家族と門下生の皆様の幸あわせと繁栄を心より願いお祈り申し上げます。

追伸
いそがしい中、英気を探して通訳と住宅、道場を気奏受提供くださり、手配してくださった、ラニー先生、美千先生、ほんとにありがとうございました。
そしてこれからも良いお付き合いよろしくお願い致します。

靖子さんおいしいステーキありがとう、これからも父とロバートさんをよろしくお願いします。

Here is the translation of the letter given to Robert Teller from Masanobu Kina's daughter, Yoko.

Ryūka 琉歌 *(*An excerpt from a Ryukyuan Song)
"The pride (fulfillment) I feel today; what can I compare it to? The joy of heart to heart contact like parents and child, the budding flower's reception of the morning dew."

I share the same wish with my father's favorite *Ryūka*.

Last year, Robert-san, Kiyoko-san, Nix Sensei and Akemi Sensei (the author's brother in law, and Kiyoko's younger sister) *came to pay respect to my father at my family altar. I was overjoyed and forgot to show my hospitality. When he visited a second time, Robert-san proposed he would like to publish a book for my father. Through your unwavering action to search my father's footprints, I realized all I can do is to tell you faithfully the memories of my father. It was very difficult to accept his death since it happened so suddenly and it took a long time to overcome the fact he was no longer with me.*

I was impressed by your devotions to learn kata from Nagira-san (Sensei Ebihara's senior student) *who succeed the last wish of Ebihara-san* (One of Master Masanobu Kina's senior students) *I saw my father in you. My father used to mention he would like to expand KARATE in the U.S.A.*

*I decided to give myself another chance to start my life with Karate (*空手人生*) with my deceased father and Higa Sensei* (Yoko's deceased karate instructor) *who are always with me.*

I can't put in words the feeling of gratitude I have. I sincerely wish you, your family, and your students happiness and prosperity.

P.S. I would like to thank Akemi Sensei and Ronnie Sensei for their time and kindness in finding my home and offering their dojo. Please keep in touch.

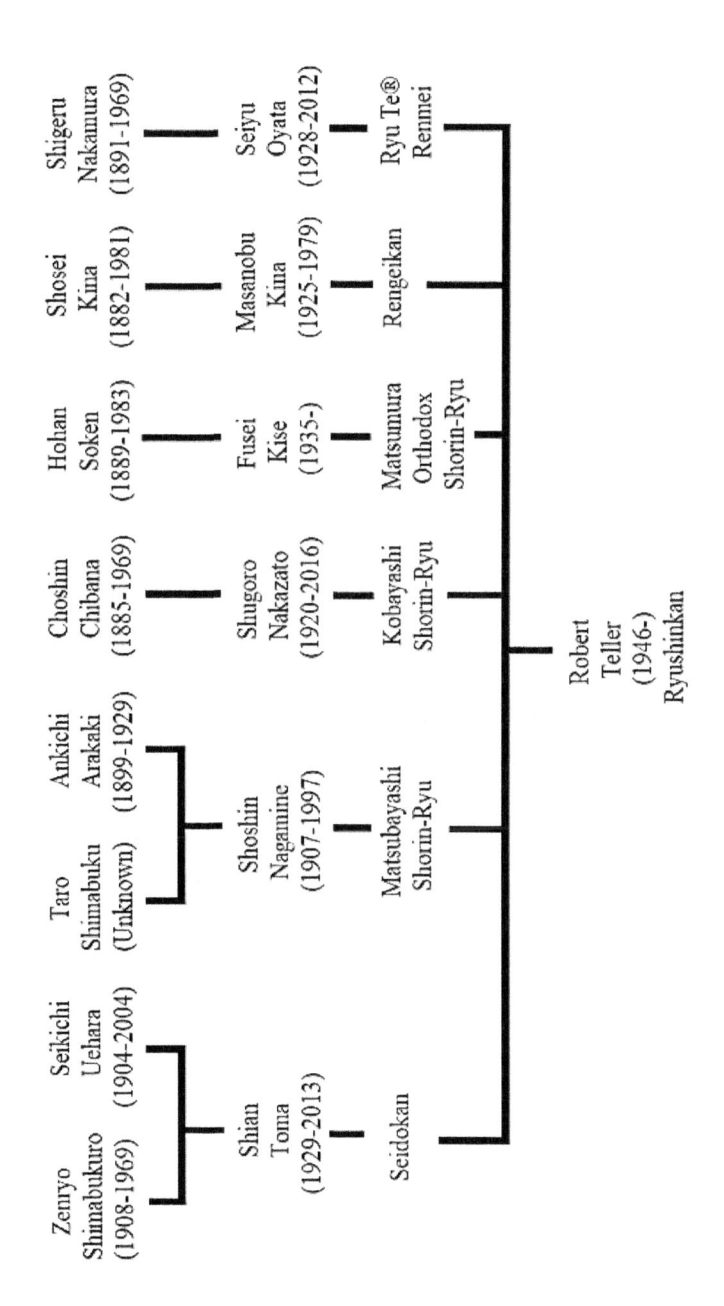

Robert Teller's Lineage

- Zenryo Shimabukuro (1908-1969)
- Seikichi Uehara (1904-2004)
  - Shian Toma (1929-2013) — Seidokan

- Taro Shimabuku (Unknown)
- Ankichi Arakaki (1899-1929)
  - Shoshin Nagamine (1907-1997) — Matsubayashi Shorin-Ryu

- Choshin Chibana (1885-1969)
  - Shugoro Nakazato (1920-2016) — Kobayashi Shorin-Ryu

- Hohan Soken (1889-1983)
  - Fusei Kise (1935-) — Matsumura Orthodox Shorin-Ryu

- Shosei Kina (1882-1981)
  - Masanobu Kina (1925-1979) — Rengeikan

- Shigeru Nakamura (1891-1969)
  - Seiyu Oyata (1928-2012) — Ryu Te® Renmei

Robert Teller (1946-) Ryushinkan

ABOUT THE AUTHOR

Robert Teller began his karate training in 1965 while stationed in Okinawa with the United States Air Force. A Vietnam veteran with over twenty-two years of active military service, he spent fifteen years in Okinawa studying under a veritable "Who's Who" of renowned karate masters. Married into an Okinawan karate family, he was exposed to styles and techniques seldom shown to outsiders.

Today he is recognized as one of the foremost authorities on traditional Okinawan karate in the United States. His articles have been featured in leading martial arts publications throughout the world. In addition to his expertise in karate, he is also an experienced teacher who enjoyed a successful career in both private and public education.